Dora's Story

Dora's Story

Dora Reisser

Dear Alex

Thanks you for all your help through so many years

Wishing you the best

Dora

Matador
9 Priory Business Park,
Wistow Road, Kibworth Beauchamp,
Leicestershire. LE8 0RX
Tel: (+44) 116 279 2299
Fax: (+44) 116 279 2277
Email: books@troubador.co.uk
Web: www.troubador.co.uk/matador

ISBN 978 1785899 836

British Library Cataloguing in Publication Data.
A catalogue record for this book is available from the British Library.

Cover design by David Beresford
Proofreading by Michael Butcher

Printed and bound in the UK by TJ International, Padstow, Cornwall
Typeset in 11pt Aldine by Troubador Publishing Ltd, Leicester, UK

Matador is an imprint of Troubador Publishing Ltd

To
My Beloved Parents
Without whom this never could have been written,
And my son, Emil, who made me write it.

'Totally compelling. That's partly because it is a story of courage and determination in the face of persecution and hardship. But also because the book is written with great clarity in a way that constantly makes you want to know what happens next. In short, I think it is a marvellous book.'

Michael Billington, *Guardian*

'We sometimes forget about the generation whose parents' lives were destroyed by Hitler and who had to reconstruct their souls amid the rubble and ruins that were all that was left of Old Europe. Dora's story is a tale of triumph over every possible adversity, a story of terror and hunger and persistence. Above all it is the tale of a survivor.'

Julian Fellowes

'The most moving and honest memoir I have ever read.'

Robert Hardy

'The extraordinary story of a prosperous family driven from its home by the ebb and flow of war could hardly be more topical. The tales of backstage confessions are endlessly entertaining. The narrative is wonderfully compelling and the story is told with real dramatic flair. It left me clamouring for more.'

Christopher Luscombe

'It's perfect, makes familiar ground unfamiliar again, many people of all ages should read it. Moving without self-pity. It prompts tears, rare in my case, at the resilience not only of Dora but her family and the greater family beyond. I know fine writing when I read it, the cumulative effect it leaves behind and the recounting of stories you won't forget'

Frank Barnard.

'Take the world and shake it.'
'I can drop you in the middle of the desert and you will find your way out.'
'Never put yourself in a ghetto.'

Emil Reisser (1902-1971)

Memories

'I will gladly forget as long as you remember.'
Emil Reisser

Oh yes, Papa, I do remember. I still can see the photo in which you wore a white suit, smoking your big fat cigar. You were powerful, strong, strict, but oh, so loving. You were the best-dressed man in my life and I had my own ways of getting all I wanted from you: teddy bears, pets, and doll after doll, big dolls, small dolls, dolls that could close their eyes and even cry. You never forgot to bring me something back from your numerous trips, chic little handbags from Paris in shining red leather, brightly-coloured fairy story books from Germany, a big blue box from Budapest containing a complete set of miniature cooking utensils – little sparkling pots and pans in which I insisted my food had to be cooked before I would eat it. It is difficult to recall exactly the first years of my life, it was so long ago, in a different world, but flashes keep appearing, like an old beloved movie.

It was in Sofia at the beginning of the war. We had a beautiful apartment – big settees covered in navy velvet, paintings on every wall, thick Turkish carpets with fringes, which Papa insisted should always lie straight.

Stanka, our maid, combed them every morning. I had to jump over them in order they were not disturbed. Everything was kept meticulously clean and orderly. We had a big gramophone with radio combined, in polished mahogany. It played classical music most of the time. I couldn't understand why, but it made me want to dance. I shared a room with my brother, Hardy. Some nights I was frightened and wanted to get to the safety of Mama, but my brother was older and knew everything.

"Dora, there is a big bear under your bed and if you put your foot down he will bite it."

He then went to sleep. I lay in my bed, for nights on end, too petrified to cry in case I woke the big bear.

Mama was beautiful: very delicate with reddish blonde hair and big brown eyes. Her skin was like alabaster. She walked under an umbrella to protect her complexion from the harsh summer sun. She wore hats at all times, usually with wide brims. I loved the way she dressed in delicate colours, never garish or loud. Her pretty little feet were always in high-heeled shoes matching the colour of her dress. Papa always used to say: "Annoushka has the best legs of all the Saltzberg daughters." Legs were always very important to Papa.

Mama loved her children. Doting on us as only a good Jewish mother could – especially my brother. I have to admit I felt a little tug at my heart when she cuddled him and not me. I never could stand being second – but in this case, whatever I did, I was always second. My brother had blonde hair, grey eyes and freckles. I followed him everywhere like a little dog. He had such an exciting life; he could go out and play in the street with other boys, while I was only allowed in the park with a nanny. One nanny was French. I didn't like her. Sometimes when I was naughty she would pinch me. She didn't stay very long since I reported everything to Mama.

I was known for my curiosity. My little red head swivelled around, right and left, and my green-brown eyes were wide-open, making sure I didn't miss a single thing. I had freckles on my nose and high cheek bones and a delicate-looking little body that was really very tough. I kept up with my brother's friends in all their rough games, although I was always very conscious not to ruin my clothes. Sometimes I had problems. My dresses were made of the finest materials, usually in white or pink, and I always had an enormous taffeta bow in my hair.

"Touch your head," Mama would say. "Right is where the bow is."

Private cars were a great rarity in Sofia, but we had two, both German of course. A cream-coloured Steyr for Mama and a black and red DKW for Papa, complete with chauffeurs – Kimon drove the DKW and Gustav the Steyr. Neither Mama nor Papa could drive. Each morning Kimon drove me to kindergarten and brought me home. Then one day, when I was all of four years old, Papa suddenly announced that I should go and come back from kindergarten by myself, in order to make me independent. I toddled off alone despite great protests from Mama. In the shortest time the entire female members of the Saltzberg family circle knew that little Dora was being made independent. Aunt Fanny, the youngest, tried to comfort Mama, but Aunt Eleanora, the middle sister, black eyes gleaming, was furious. Thank God, Aunt Sophie, the eldest, had immigrated to Brooklyn. Grandmother Rachel was not informed in case she died of an apoplexy – she adored Papa but this time he would not have easily been forgiven.

The kindergarten was not far away but I had to cross an enormous square, dominated by the Russian Cathedral. I had peeped in a few times and had been fascinated by the mystique, the unfamiliar smell of incense, and the golden icons shimmering amongst ornaments studded with brightly coloured stones. It was both an enchanting and frightening place for me, but after the experience of the bear under my bed I had trained myself to be brave. I arrived at the kindergarten safely but there was a slight wind blowing when I came out to go home. As I re-crossed the square by the Cathedral it swiftly developed into a raging gale, as happens in that part of the world. Everything that was not fixed firmly to the ground took off, including me. I was swept up in the air, experiencing an extremely unusual sensation – I was flying! Thank God, a kind man noticed my predicament and pulled me down.

"Where do you live?"

"1, Ulitsa Titscher." Mama had made sure that at least had been driven firmly into my head.

He put me on his shoulder and took me home, where Mama was waiting anxiously to take me in her arms.

That was the last time I was sent alone to kindergarten to be made independent, and the entire family gave a sigh of relief. Papa was rebuked for several days, but he was a great charmer and could make jokes out of everything and the incident was quickly forgotten. The others may not have realised it, but Papa had seen what was happening in Germany and was trying to prepare me for a far greater storm.

2

Childhood in Sofia

Sofia is the capital of Bulgaria, a small eastern European country that had been ruled by the Turks for more than 400 years before it was liberated by Tsar Alexander II in 1877. The Tsar promptly established a kingdom with his nephew, another Alexander, as king. Austria, Germany and England, feared the creation of a strong Russian satellite in so sensitive a region and insisted that the provinces of Thrace and Macedonia should be detached and given to Serbia and Greece. This was to cause bitter wars and ultimate tragedy in the following years. King Alexander's reign was brief, he was deposed in 1886, and the new kingdom was left without a king. The problem was that Bulgaria had no native aristocracy from which a monarch could be found. The National Assembly, in almost a fairy story fashion, designated three prominent citizens to travel Europe in search of a suitable candidate. Their choice ultimately fell on a German princeling, Ferdinand of Saxe-Coburg-Gotha, grandson of the last king of France and nephew of Queen Victoria of England – most of the royal blood in Europe came from her at that time.

Ferdinand was vain and pompous but transformed Sofia from a muddy Ottoman town into a modern

European city, with boulevards, parks, museums, theatres, a university and opera house. He became more Bulgarian than the Bulgarians in his desire to recover the lost provinces of Macedonia and Thrace, and impetuously led his country into two Balkan wars before allying himself with Germany and Austria in 1914. He was forced to abdicate following their defeat and was succeeded by his son, Boris.

My father, Emil Jacob Reisser, was born in 1902, a Jew in Stuttgart, Germany. The earliest photo I have of him is in his elementary school class when he was about eight. One of the boys holds a small blackboard with 1910 scrawled upon it. Most of the boys look apprehensive, probably it is the first time they have had their picture taken, but Emil stands proudly plumb in the middle of the group, staring defiantly at the camera with his arm flung around the shoulder of the boy next to him. He is fair-haired, strong and sturdy, and looks every bit as German as the boys around him. He had no understanding with his father, but he loved his mother, Dorothea, deeply. She died when he was fifteen and he would name me, his daughter, after her. He left Germany shortly after his mother's death and went east to seek his fortune as many middle Europeans did at that time. In an unexploited and unsophisticated country such as Bulgaria, there was a lot of money to be made. Through hard work, determination and quick wits, he eventually became a very rich man. He built and developed properties, printed newspapers and text books; in fact anything that was printable except money.

Through his contacts in Germany he introduced the first coloured printing into Bulgaria. He was influential, gregarious and popular; he wore the best clothes, made for him by Rosenbaum, the court-appointed tailor, and took morning rides in the Boris Garden, the beautiful park in the centre of Sofia. He had as many Gentile friends as Jews, and was even on good terms with Eugen Rümelin, the long-serving German Ambassador. When Crown Prince Simeon was born, Emil Reisser was invited to the palace as an honoured guest. He had his full share of beautiful women, but when the time came to settle down and have children, he turned some of his extraordinary energy into finding a suitable wife.

"Have fun, but at home you need a nice Jewish girl."

There were four nice girls in the Saltzberg family. The Saltzbergs had been wealthy. Grandfather Joseph, an accountant, had held a high office under the Tsar before he had been driven out of Kiev by the Revolution. He was shy and genteel, in contrast to Grandmother Rachel who was fierce and somewhat eccentric. She smoked Turkish cigarillos continuously – visitors had to present their visiting cards on a silver tray and were refused entry if she considered them ugly. For a while the family lived a comfortable and cultured life in Constantinople, until the money ran out. They ended up in the beautiful little city of Varna on the Black Sea, where the cultured life continued on a more modest scale. Grandfather Joseph could play practically any instrument and all four girls were skilled musicians. Sophie and Fanny played the violin, Eleanora the flute, and Anna the piano. There was a chamber concert nearly every evening. It was an extremely close-knit and religious family: candles were lit and prayers said every Friday. No one was permitted to intrude inside the circle without the approval of Grandmother Rachel, who held a strong grip over her daughters while doting on Danny, her only son.

But an intruder duly arrived in the shape of Emil Reisser. It happened at an embassy ball in Varna. The local high society had been invited, including Jews. In Bulgaria at that time, Jews were treated like everyone else. Emil saw Anna, danced with her and knew straight away that she was just what he had been looking for. He contrived to get a ruby ring from her finger, which he promised to return to her at her home the following day. Anna was shocked. How could a gentleman do such a thing? But when she told her mother what had happened, Rachel wasn't shocked, but thrilled. Sophie had found Mr Leon Cornfeld, a Romanian actor and impresario, in Constantinople, married him, and had soon presented Rachel with Bernie, her first grandchild; but there were still three more daughters to go. They were beautiful but not all that young. Twenty-two was considered old for marriage at that time.

The next morning, when the doorbell rang, Anna was hiding under the big bed that she shared with Fanny. She was painfully shy and very delicate. She was hardly allowed to do any work about the house. The other members of the family would always help her because they worried about her health and thought she could not cope with problems. She remained under the bed until her mother summoned her out. Mr Saltzberg met Mr Reisser and was definitely against the match: he had lost his eldest daughter to a Romanian actor, and now, his most loving Annoushka, to a German Jew? He couldn't accept it. But Mr Reisser had used all his charm on Mrs Saltzberg, knowing that was the way to Anna. Mrs Saltzberg liked Mr Reisser, she liked his cigars and considered him handsome, and that was that.

The young couple went out a few times accompanied by Rachel, but this was not to Emil's liking, and they were married in a matter of months. As it happened, the other daughters followed shortly after. Fanny, the most progressive, who worked as a secretary, married Salomon Aladgem, a plumbing engineer of Spanish descent. Again Mr Saltzberg did not approve. A plumber was bad enough – but a Sephardic Jew as well? The Saltzbergs were Ashkenazi. He was better pleased when Eleanora married into the Hertz family, who were noted for their physicists. But his biggest disappointment came when his son, Danny, fell in love with a Christian girl. That was too much. Danny was forbidden to marry her. The poor young man locked himself in his room for many days and would not talk or eat, and over the years became more and more strange.

However, Emil had got the woman he wanted and was very happy. He constricted his social activities, still having little flirtations but being very discreet about them. His home was sacrosanct. That home was a first floor apartment in a block he had built, complete with a garage for his cars, near the Boris

Garden, the most exclusive area in Sofia, close to the Royal Palace. Anna slowly but surely settled into Emil's exuberant existence. They went regularly to the best restaurants and the opera. She captivated her husband's mixed social circle with her beauty and elegance and was welcomed everywhere. She was honest and had tremendous patience with her high-spirited husband, giving him stability. When Hardy was born in 1934, Anna was showered with presents. When Deborah arrived in 1938, Emil was enjoying a lucky streak at the casino. He burst into the hospital and threw money all over the bed, proclaiming: "Annoushka, this is a lucky child!" Emil was always larger than life.

My parents created an ambience of great happiness in our home. We spoke German, French Yiddish and Bulgarian, all mixed together, which made it very noisy and very lively. Every summer we went for a long holiday to our villa in the country. It was close to Vrana, King Boris's summer palace, about fifteen kilometres outside the city. We would often see King Boris riding with his smartly uniformed entourage. The peasants cheered and bowed, while he acknowledged their loyal devotion with a gracious wave. We knew his face so well; his photo was hung prominently on the wall in our sitting room in Sofia.

Then one summer my brother and I were deposited in the country with only a nanny and Stanka, our maid, to take care of us. Papa and Mama came to see us at the weekends – Mama beautiful as ever, arriving at exactly the time she had promised and dressed to utter perfection. But Papa didn't always come. Business or something else seemed to keep him back.

When we returned to Sofia the atmosphere had changed. People came in and out of our apartment. People I hadn't seen before. They hung their coats in the corridor.

"Mama, why do they all have yellow stars?"

No answer. They looked pretty.

"Mama, why can't I have one on my coat?"

"Because Papa doesn't like it."

That was enough for me not to like it too.

The visitors sat in the sitting room and whispered, listening fearfully to the radio – I didn't understand why they didn't listen to their own radios but nobody discussed anything with us children. Mama and Papa continued to go out nearly every evening. We were given firm instructions that if we heard a loud shrilling noise we were not to be frightened, but to put on our dressing gowns and follow Nanny down to the cellar along with the occupants of other apartments. Papa would be shortly with us. The night came – Papa and Mama were out – when a terrifying, shrilling sound shook the building and went through our bodies. Nanny bundled us up in blankets and hurried us down to the cellar. Everybody there was very quiet, listening fearfully to the explosions and the whistling noises up above. We had no idea what would happen next. I was almost paralysed with fear. I did everything I could to prevent myself crying. All of a sudden there was a noise on the stairs above us.

"Dora! Hardy! Are you there?"

"Papa! Papa! Papa!"

There he was. My adorable strong father and there was nothing to be afraid of. No obstacle could prevent him getting to us. He held me close to his breast. Everybody began talking to him. Asking him what was going on outside? What was happening? How did he ever get through with all the bombs falling around him?

"It looks bad. The Americans and British are bombing Sofia."

A few days later the situation got even worse when we heard that King Boris was dead. It was almost impossible to believe. He died suddenly, without any warning, after returning from a meeting with Hitler in Germany. Everyone was shocked and frightened. I heard the grown-ups whispering that the King must have been poisoned A few days later we stood in the dense crowd as King Boris's coffin was borne through the streets on a gun carriage. Elaborately uniformed Hussars marched at his side, their drawn sabres resting on their shoulders. Behind came Queen Giovanna and Prince Cyril, the Regent, and many men in German uniforms. The people all around us were crying and Mama was crying too. A new photo began to appear everywhere; a photo of a man with a little moustache, like Charlie Chaplin but with a frightening face. He did not smile as King Boris had done. Mama didn't laugh. Papa didn't talk. My questions went unanswered.

I learnt many years later that King Boris had done all he could to ensure that his small country, wedged between Germany and Russia, remained neutral. 'When horses kick each other in the stable, donkeys get hurt' was one of Papa's favourite sayings, and the King was eventually forced into an alliance with that frightening man who did not smile. Papa had taken great care that I was not aware of them, but anti-Jewish laws had been passed in 1940, as vicious and stringent as those in Germany. But they were not strictly enforced. Though Bulgaria had its own fascist party, the aptly named 'Ratniks', there was no tradition of anti-Semitism in Bulgaria. Bulgarian Jews were not rich: there were only 56 Jewish lawyers and 84 Jewish doctors and not a single Jewish banker in all of Sofia. Most Jews earned their living through hard physical labour, or they were small merchants, pushcart vendors, owners of little shops. They dressed like everyone else – there were no Hasidics with big black hats and curls. The majority of Bulgarian Jews did not eat kosher food and worked on Saturdays. They were the most assimilated in all Europe. When Eichmann had sent his own envoy, SS Haupsturmführer Theodore Dannecker, to Bulgaria to begin the transportation of Jews in February 1943, Metropolitan Kyril, head of the Orthodox Church, threatened to lie across the tracks to prevent the trains moving. "Wherever they go, I go!" he said. Intellectuals, writers, the unions of lawyers and doctors, members of the Senate united in protest, and not a single Jewish subject of King Boris was deported or suffered an unnatural death.

But the 12,000 Jews of Thrace and Macedonia, conquered territories which Bulgaria had agreed to administer for the Nazis, were not so fortunate. Dannecker ensured they were brutally deported in sealed boxcars, crammed so tight that they could do nothing but stand, treated worse than animals without air and water, enduring a moving hell for days on end, until they were finally loaded on ships on the Danube to be taken on to Vienna, Poland and death. I recently discovered a poem a young man, working in a Jewish labour gang, wrote after watching the trains pass:

And a car to a car is chained
And together they heavily move.
The faces are yellow and scarring
Tortured birds are the eyes.
The dresses are worn and threadbare
Frostbitten they are. Wet are the cheeks
And if you forgot
May your eyes rot
That saw that sight
When trains dark of sorrow
Dragged Jews to their death.

Papa had seen the trains too. He had been born a German, and knew that his family would automatically be counted as German, not Bulgarian – they would be without the King's protection. He was determined to do everything in his power to save his little family from such a terrible fate.

Now King Boris was dead the anti-Jewish laws were more ruthlessly enforced. Jews were no longer allowed to own property, businesses, or radios – they could not use the telephone without special authorisation. Papa got round this by pretending Leo, his non-Jewish foreman, was the owner of his various businesses. Leo was Papa's friend. Papa was not like the other Jews. He spoke perfect German – he passed as a German. Even though his old acquaintance, Rümelin, had been replaced by Adolf-Heinz Beckerle, a fanatic anti-Semite and rabid Nazi, he still had contacts at the German embassy and obtained false documents, stating that he was an Aryan. That meant that he could move freely, ignore the curfew, listen to the BBC on his radio and inform his Jewish acquaintances of the latest situation. He helped them financially as much as he could and even assisted some in crossing the Turkish border to safety in Constantinople.

Half of Bulgaria's 50,000 Jews lived in Sofia and most of them were being forcibly removed – the men to labour camps, the rest to ghettos. Mama's entire family, the Saltzbergs, the Aladgems and the Hertzes were sent to a ghetto in the distant town of Shumen. Aunt Fanny told me later that they were only allowed to bring one suitcase each; a fortunate few had neighbours with whom they could entrust their other belongings, the majority lost everything. They had heard the terrible rumours of the camps in Poland, and Aunt Fanny packed a separate little suitcase for my cousins, Lily and Nina, in case they were separated. They received orders to be at the main railway station at a certain time and everybody obeyed, waiting patiently on the platform. They were put on normal trains, but each time the train stopped,

Aunt Fanny dreaded they would be ordered out and put on a cattle truck to Poland.

Papa had refused to live in ghettos all his life, and used all his influence to keep us in Sofia. Even so, two large suitcases were packed and prepared in the hall.

3

Our Wanderings Begin

The British and Americans continued their bombardments, they became more and more terrifying, until one night the whole sky seemed to be on fire. Papa had had enough.

"Anna. Get the children ready quickly. The chauffeur is waiting. We are going to the villa at Vrana."

I grabbed my favourite doll, the one whose eyes closed and opened, and waited fearfully at the door. We clambered into Papa's red DKW, which Gustav was driving, and a nightmare began. All of Sofia seemed to be fleeing the city. Everything was burning, there was no transport. People were pushing their belongings in carts or pulling them on beds behind them. They tried to stop the only car on the road but Papa was determined to save his loved ones. He became ruthless, in a way I'd never seen, and pushed them off violently, yelling at the chauffeur.

"Drive! Drive, Gustav I tell you! Don't look! Drive!"

He threw blankets over our heads to prevent us becoming even more frightened, but I peeped out and saw a sight that has remained with me all my life – faces and hands, pressing and banging against the car's windows; terrified faces, screaming and yelling. Streets on fire, hot stifling air, everything burning. The only reassuring sound was Papa's voice:

"Drive, Gustav. Don't stop. I tell you drive!"

What was happening to my beautiful world?

We reached the villa at last and Papa stayed with us throughout the remainder of the night. He found a litter of motherless kittens and took them into the house. Hardy and I watched as he tried to feed them by dipping a piece of cloth into a bowl of milk and dripping little drops into their tiny mouths. I looked at my father and wondered at his patience and love. He stayed up all night to keep those kittens alive. He was so tender to them, but how hard he had been to the people in Sofia in his determination to save us.

Morning came. Papa kissed both of us. "Be good to your mother. I will be back soon. I'm going to the printing house to pick up the suitcases with the gold printing plates, they are very valuable. Then I have to meet Leo at the apartment. That's the last thing I have to do. We will be rich and safe in Turkey." He turned to Mama, who was looking paler than ever. "Don't worry. I have the papers – I am a fully Aryan German." He smiled, although I could see it wasn't a smile, and gave her a bundle of money. "Use this if you need it. Don't use the buttons unless you have to."

I didn't understand what he meant at the time.

Mama went down with Papa to the car, where Gustav was waiting. Hardy and I watched from the window as Mama kissed Papa goodbye and then turned and clasped the chauffeur's hand. I had never seen her do that before.

Papa waved to us from the back window until the car turned out of the drive.

One day passed – two days – three. We had no more milk. The kittens died one by one. Hardy buried them side by side in the garden. At night we heard fearful explosions and saw the flashes in the sky as the bombardment of Sofia continued. Mama's desperation was almost unbearable. Papa was under those bombs. If only he would come back. He would tell her what to do – how to keep her children safe. We all slept together in one bed at night and were not allowed to leave her side throughout the day. We were glued to her. She waited, dreading something terrible had happened.

At last, on the fourth morning, the car reappeared at the end of the drive. Papa had come back as he had said he would. We ran excitedly and joyfully towards it. It stopped. The door opened. Leo got out.

All three of us were stunned.

"Where is my husband?"

"Let us go into the house, Frau Reisser, where we can talk."

We went inside, full of apprehension. Leo spoke very quietly.

"When I got to your apartment, Frau Reisser, the Gestapo were waiting. Emil arrived and they arrested him immediately. They knew everything about him. He was a Jew pretending to be an Aryan with false papers and was helping Jews escape. None of his talk could get him out of it. They took him away. I've spent days trying to find out where they took him, but nobody seems to know. I'm sorry – he must have been taken to a camp or shot."

Mama said nothing but looked at him with disbelieving eyes.

Leo took three yellow stars out of his pocket and laid them on the table. "You and the children had better wear these now."

Mama's face had changed to stone. "Thank you, Leo." She went outside and whispered something to Gustav, the chauffeur, who was waiting by the DKW. Leo followed her, got into Papa's car and Gustav drove it away.

Mama sat at the table and looked at the yellow stars. "Emil didn't want us to wear them."

We stood beside her silently. She remained sitting there a long, long time with tears running down her cheeks. At last, she slowly reached out, took our hands and kissed them and put them to her heart. All her tender Yiddish words of endearment came tumbling out of her. We stared at the yellow stars – we didn't touch them. They were like hot iron. Mama got up with a determined face.

"I am packing now."

Night had almost fallen when we heard the car coming back up the drive. The chauffeur got out and came into the house.

Mama clasped his hand, "Gustav, thank you for coming back. Tell me what happened."

Gustav was a simple man and hesitated, trying to find the right words. "Frau Reisser, I wouldn't stay here in your place."

"I know. We have already packed. But tell me what happened."

"When we arrived near the apartment, Herr Reisser told me park in an alley and stay in the car and keep it out of sight. He said he wouldn't be long. When he didn't come, I went to the corner and saw your husband with Leo and the Gestapo. Leo must have been waiting with them for him to arrive. When they took him away I heard Herr Reisser call over his shoulder, 'Leo, take care of them and give them everything. Tell them I will see them soon.' Leo came to the car, told me to drive him home and took the two suitcases."

Mama was suddenly no longer a delicate flower. She came to a decision at once.

"We must get into the mountains – as far away as possible – somewhere where we can hide and nobody will know who we are. Do you know anywhere where we can go?"

Gustav thought for a moment. "I'll take you to the village where I was born. I'll find you a place there." He took the big suitcases, Hardy struggled with a little one, Mama took her handbag and I my doll.

It was another terrifying drive, mother sat between us on the back seat, clutching our hands so tightly, endeavouring to reassure us with every fibre of her being. At first we kept to the main road. We could hardly see anything with only the side lights on. Then, all at once, a barrier came out of the darkness in front of us. It was good Gustav was driving so slowly otherwise he would have crashed into it. The car shuddered to a halt whilst a bright torch was shone into our faces.

Some soldiers came out of the darkness.

"Who are you? Where are you going? Have you a permit?"

Thank God, they were Bulgarian voices not German.

Gustav produced the papers that Papa had obtained from the German Embassy. One of the soldiers, a sergeant, examined them with his torch.

"This only permits you to travel in the Sofia district. What are you doing here?"

Gustav was at a loss for words. Mama wound down her window. The torch's beam swung on to her face. She smiled. She still looked so beautiful.

"We are taking the children to my sister in the country to escape the bombs. It is terrible in Sofia."

I don't know if she had charmed the sergeant, but he nodded sympathetically. "Very well; have a safe journey." He gave a signal and the barrier was raised.

We had only driven a few kilometres before Gustav swung the car to the right.

"We had better avoid the main road. There will be more checkpoints. We may not be so lucky next time. But the roads will be bad. They are not really roads at all."

He was right. We were tossed up and down and from side to side. Even my little head nearly bounced up to the roof. As we began to climb into the mountains it got worse. At times we hit rocks or felt them scrape on the bottom of the car beneath us. Gustav stopped once to refill the tank from the spare cans that Papa had insisted he always carried. At last, as dawn was breaking, we arrived at a village. Most of the houses looked very small and poor, but there were a few bigger ones around the square. Gustav stopped the car beneath some trees and went into one of the bigger houses. We waited fearfully until he returned with a short, broad-shouldered man. He looked dirty and had shifty eyes. Gustav got back into the car. The man got in also and sat next to Gustav in the front. He smelt of onions and sweat.

"Frau Reisser, this is my cousin. He has somewhere quiet outside the village where you can stay."

We drove a short distance before we turned off the road onto a track. It led through the trees to a clearing in which was a wooden hut with a fence in front. When we entered it we realised that it had only one room.

Mama took it in with her sad eyes. "That's fine."

"He wants 1000 leva and you can stay as long as you want. Wood for the stove is outside in the yard. Someone will bring you food once a week. It will be left by the gate. He will show you the stone by the gate under which you will leave 50 leva every Monday."

Mama took the money out of her handbag and gave it to the squat man. He took it and carefully counted it before he nodded and went out of the hut.

"Gustav, I have one more thing to ask you." She gave him a piece of paper. "These are the names of all my family in the ghetto at Shumen. I must get a message to them to let them know where we are."

He took the paper and folded it carefully into his top pocket. "I will try, Frau Reisser. But it may take time."

Mama was wearing a double-breasted coat. She tore off one of the big buttons and pulled away the material to reveal a glittering coin, a gold thaler, with the head of Maria Theresa stamped upon it. She gave it to him.

"Thank you for everything. I don't think we will see each other again. God bless you."

"God bless you too," he mumbled. "All of you."

He turned and was gone and we were all alone.

Mama did her best to smile. "Let's make a home."

4

The Hut in the Trees

We began to clean straight away. We had to pump water from the well, and all too soon discovered that the toilet was simply a hole in a shed outside. The smell was unbearable and the flies were even worse. Nevertheless Mama did everything she could to keep our new home in perfect order, insisting that we still kept our table manners, even whilst we sat at the primitive table eating nothing but bread.

"We are the lucky ones," she would tell us.

The ugliness around us didn't seem to matter as long as Mama was there. I can only marvel at her bravery and strength. Every night throughout that autumn and winter she sat alone with her small children with darkness all around her. She had no idea where Papa was: whether he was alive or in some terrible camp. She had no news – not even rumours. We spoke to no one. We saw no one. We never went out. Mama told us never to go into the village. We looked different – it wouldn't be safe for us. We watched autumn and winter passing through the ragged, flimsy curtains. I was so cold. Bread, milk, cheese and sometimes eggs were left by the stone each Monday. Potatoes and other vegetables were growing in yard behind the hut. We didn't starve but we were always hungry. Each week we hoped for news from the family in Schuman, but nothing came.

I had only one question, "When is Papa coming? He promised he would."

"Soon, Dorchika, soon."

One day I stopped asking. I could see the pain it caused in my mother's eyes

We had no toys, apart from my doll, and no books. Mama would make up stories for us, or tell us of the happy times she had spent in the great city of Constantinople, she never called it Istanbul. She would tell us of her oldest sister Fanny and our cousin Benno, who had gone to live in that wonderful promised land of America. She taught us to sew – Hardy was much better at it than me. She also invented all sorts of games to keep us amused. My favourite was when she dressed me in Hardy's clothes and he in mine. I had to be the boy and Hardy was the girl. I was so delighted to have mastery over my big brother for once. The sordid little hut was briefly filled with laughter and some sort of happiness, but not for long. Spring came at last. One morning, Mama took me to the small stream close to the house. We sat and looked at the shining stones and listened to the bubbling water. It was beautiful, everything was being reborn; at that moment the world seemed at peace. Lilac trees were in blossom, Mama always loved their fragrance. We picked some and took them back to the hut. But when we got there Hardy came running towards us, with blood on his face. He was crying.

"Mama, I'm sorry. I went to the village and the boys threw stones at me."

Peace disappeared in an instant. We were alone again amongst people who hated us.

Some nights later we heard boots running through the trees outside, then shouts and cries and the sharp crack of rifle shots. We trembled as Mama held us tightly to her, clasping our little hands, as if she would never let them go. Where they Germans or Partisans? Had they come for us? They were more terrifying than any bears. But nobody bothered with our little dark hut.

The following Monday there was no food by the stone. We looked anxiously up at Mama. What would we do now? There was nothing but the vegetables growing in the yard. We had to live off them. I have no idea how long we did, it seemed like weeks but it could have been days. Then late one evening, as we were sitting at the rough table drinking potato soup, there was a soft tap on the door. We froze and looked at each other, terrified. Nobody had ever knocked before. Had they come for us after all?

"Anna! Are you there?"

The door pushed open. We saw a bearded peasant.

It took a moment to recognise Uncle Salomon.

Tears began to run down Mama's cheeks. "Wonders do happen. They really do."

Salomon enfolded her in his arms and she clung onto him, sobbing with relief, as if she had found a rock at the point of drowning in a tempestuous sea. Eventually she pulled away and summoned all her courage.

"Have you news of Emil?" she asked fearfully.

Salomon shook his head. "There is no time for talk. You must pack and leave straight away. Communist partisans are in the area. I have a horse and cart outside."

We asked no more questions and were ready in an instant. Mama was wearing her coat with the missing button. He looked at us and shook his head. Even after months in the hut we still looked like the bourgeoisie.

"You will have to hide in the straw beneath the tarpaulin until we have passed through the village."

Salomon grabbed the suitcases and we hurried out behind him and clambered into the cart. A sullen, red-faced farmer was drinking vodka from a bottle with one hand whilst holding the reins of two weary-looking horses in the other. Empty bottles were strewn on the floor of the cart around him.

Mama looked questioningly at Uncle Salomon, who spoke in Yiddish.

"He is the only one I could persuade to take me. He keeps getting lost. That is why it has taken me so long."

Uncle Salomon had just covered us with a nasty smelling tarpaulin when I remembered.

"I forgot my doll. I can't leave her behind."

Salomon ran back into the hut and put her safely in my arms.

"Now not another sound until we are clear of the village."

The farmer flicked his whip and we began to move. I had never been down the track since that day we had arrived so many months before. This little hut and yard had been my entire world. It was now a moonlit night and when we passed through the village I couldn't resist peeking out of the side of the tarpaulin. I wished I hadn't. Bodies were hanging from the trees around the square with tongues hanging from their distorted faces. I think one of them was Gustav's cousin.

5

Shumen

We travelled for several hours before Uncle Salomon thought it was safe to stop. He told Mama that the British and Americans were in Italy and were preparing to land in France, and the Russians were advancing in the east. He explained they had not got the message until the winter, and he had been forbidden to leave the ghetto. It was only now, when it looked as if the Germans were going to lose the war that the government had slightly eased the restrictions against the Jews, and he had managed to get out of Shumen. He had managed to hire this farmer and his cart with money that Papa had left with him. All the family were in Shumen, safe and well and our cousins were looking forward to playing with us. Shumen was in the east of the country and it would take us a week or so to get there in the cart, longer if the drunken fool kept losing his way.

It must have taken enormous courage for Uncle Salomon to leave his own family and travel across the war-torn country; he most probably saved our lives. I've often wondered why he did it – I always suspected that he had a soft spot for Mama. I can't remember much of that journey. I slept most of the time in the straw beneath the tarpaulin with Mama's arms around me and my arms around my doll.

When at last we arrived in Shumen there was an unbelievable reunion with the entire family, the Aladgems, the Hertzes and the Saltzbergs, full of happiness, tears and laughter. They all talked at once and argued who had the most news to tell. "*Wir besprechen de lage*" was on everyone's tongue. "We will sit down and discuss the situation". They discussed the situation again and again. And when they got tired and had no answers, they decided to discuss it again the next day. Nobody mentioned Papa. They were too afraid to say what they thought, but when the others had gone, Mama and Fanny talked long into the night, asking questions that neither could answer.

We moved in to a small, simple house with Uncle Salomon, Aunt Fanny and Lily and Nina. It was a mansion compared to the hut, but was very cramped for the seven of us. We ate our meals on a table outside and there was no bathroom or toilet. The rest of the family were renting rooms in a larger house. I don't know how they managed to pay rent, but somehow they did. There were hardly any men in the ghetto, they were all away on working gangs, mending roads and building defences. The old Jews and women and children were more or less left on their own to take care of themselves.

Hardy and I settled down with our cousins very well. Lily was only a few months older than me and Nina was two years younger. We were so happy to have someone else to play with. There was a Jewish school but we did not attend. Shumen was so different to Sofia. It was an old Ottoman city with minarets seemingly on every corner, and we heard Muslim calls to prayer throughout the day. A little stream with a wooden bridge was all that separated us from the Muslim part of the town. There was no high wall surrounding the Ghetto, only that little stream, which was choked with all manner of rubbish and sewage and smelt revolting. It couldn't possibly cope with the huge number of refugees and was buzzing with flies. The strong sun didn't help either. A favourite game we children played was to go to the bridge and spit down into the stream – whoever spat furthest won. We were never allowed to cross it, so we used our imagination to make up stories about the secret city on the other side – where people wore different clothes and said different prayers and lived different lives. Hardy was a boy and five years older and always knew best, but we girls continually challenged him.

Food was sparse, perhaps the grown-ups went short, but we children never really went hungry. Nevertheless, we invented all sorts of ways to supplement our rations. I always ate my food very, very slowly. When the others had all finished, I always made sure I had some left. Sometimes I gave a little morsel to Hardy, but the last bite was always mine. We were continually looking for extra food. We lived next door to a Rabbi who had a much bigger and better garden than we did. It was overflowing with figs and grapes and other delights. They looked very tempting. In our minds it was quite clear to us that the Rabbi should share whatever he had with us. We informed the Rabbi's son of our conclusion, but to our surprise he didn't agree with us whatsoever.

On the contrary, he reported us to his father, who told us off and made in quite clear that nobody should dare venture into his garden, and made the wooden fence, that separated his abundant garden from our meagre one, more secure. We sat down and discussed it like a parliamentary meeting. There was no opposition – they wouldn't have had a chance anyway:

'Has he got more money that he should have a better garden?'

'Was he just lucky that he had a better garden?'

'What has he done to deserve a better garden?'

'Whatever it may be, we want some of his better garden'.

We decided that we should do something about it. At the end of our garden was a little hut that contained the rubbish tins. The fence wasn't secured there. We crept down, while the grown-ups weren't looking, pulled the loose planks apart, crawled through and had a feast. It was a big supplement to our meagre rations. The Rabbi had so much he never noticed.

We four children slept in one room and the grown-ups in another. The mosquitoes ate us up every night, being close to the stinking stream didn't help. They took a particular delight in me. I was covered in bites, which used to itch dreadfully. All Mama could do was to spit on her finger, tap gently on the bites and promise they would get better. I believed her. I believed everything she said. My poor doll had been hugged so much that she was continually leaking sawdust. Mama patched her up so many times before giving me a little pillow to hug in bed at night instead. I have slept with a little pillow ever since – I can't sleep without it – and my doll is still intact and still stares at me as I write this, with her glass eyes that have seen so much.

Then one day a newspaper arrived out of nowhere. Spread across the front page was a picture of three men sitting together. People were shouting, "Churchill, Stalin and Roosevelt are united. The war will soon be over!" They were crying, 'Freedom!' 'We will be free!' 'Now we can go home!' Yellow stars were torn off. Everyone was talking, singing, packing: ecstatic with the oxygen of freedom.

Papa! Papa! Papa! You will come back. We will be back together again. Back to our beautiful home, back to our comfortable, safe life. The bad dream is over. The clouds of misery are blowing away and the sun's rays are shining through. Mama would rule her little domain again.

She took both me and Hardy in her arms.

"Now we will go home. We will go back to our old life."

6

Back to Sofia

It wasn't the Sofia I remembered. It was full of Russian soldiers and scarred with bombing. We went to stay with Aunt Fanny and Uncle Salomon until we could move back into our apartment. But our dreams were soon shattered. It never happened. All the Jews were given back their homes except us. Our apartment had been allocated to a high-ranking Russian officer. The new authorities considered us Germans because Papa was a German. They ignored the fact that Mama had been born in Russia and Hardy and I were Bulgarian. It seemed we couldn't win. We had been persecuted by the Germans because we were Jews and now by the Communists because we were supposedly Germans.

There was nothing for us but to continue staying with Uncle Salomon and Aunt Fanny in their small flat near the old Jewish quarter. They were very kind, but we constantly felt as if we were intruding, clambering over each other in the cramped rooms. We longed to have our own proper home

"Oh, Papa, where are you?"

Many nights I cried myself to sleep, still missing his warm, protective hand on my shoulder. Mama was still the most loving mother in the world. She must have suffered terribly – not knowing where Papa was or what was going to happen to us, but never for a moment did she let us know her worries. But I knew. Time takes its toll, nerves get frailer. Papa had always insured that she had never had to ask for anything, but now we no longer had money or a home. I caught snatches of conversation, in hushed voices, but money was never mentioned when children were around. Mama was still beautiful, she wasn't short of admirers, but she would only go out if she were accompanied by Fanny and Salomon. Whenever she did go out, I waited impatiently for her to come back. I wanted to make sure she hadn't forgotten Papa, to whom she belonged.

My two cousins were the beauties in the eyes of the rest of the family. I wasn't sure if my mother shared that opinion but she never said otherwise. Lily and Nina's hair developed into thick beautiful curls, mine seemed to get thinner and thinner, until Mama decided to cut it very short to give it a chance to recuperate. I didn't understand from what. My freckles seemed to be more dominant on my face than ever before. No lemon juice or cucumber could remove them, and the lemon juice made my face burn. I took the pain, trying to smile, hoping it would give me a clear complexion like Lily and Nina.

Hardy, of course, was the only boy and could do no wrong. He was an expert at getting things he wasn't allowed to have and doing the things he wasn't allowed to do, but we learned from him fast. At night, when the grown-ups were out, we played all sorts of forbidden games. For example, getting into the locked cabinet where Uncle Salomon kept his sweet sticky drinks. We filled our tummies, even though it practically made us sick, and then we filled little perfume bottles with egg, chocolate and cherry liqueur, being very careful not to spill any evidence on the floor. Another game was 'Sunken Ships'. The furniture was turned upside down and transformed into shipwrecks and we jumped from one to the other, to the great detriment of Uncle Salomon's tables, sofas and chairs. But my favourite was when Lily and Nina would lie on the floor motionless, and I would dance between them to an old scratched record of Debussy's *Claire de Lune*. They were supposed to be sleeping flowers and I was a fairy, and they could only awake when I stamped my foot close to them. I loved the music and often would forget about them entirely, enjoying my dance so much.

"When are you going to stamp your foot, Dora?" Lily would enquire at last.

"Soon, soon," but I continued with my dance.

"When? When?" Nina would plead.

"Not yet. I haven't finished casting my spell."

Eventually they got up in disgust. "We are not going to play this game again."

But they always did.

We were four strong-minded children, living in close proximity, and it was hardly surprising that fighting broke out frequently. The girls knew that if they got to my head and pulled my hair they would win. I was petrified to lose even two hairs – I had so little – and I imagined that if the fight continued I would be left with bald patches: they would pull out the roots and they would never grow again. In contrast, if I was lucky and managed to pull Lily's hair first, I sometimes ended up with a thick bunch in my hand, which she never missed at all.

One good thing about Uncle Salomon's flat was that it was right next door to a cinema and Hardy would take us girls to the special children's shows. We loved the cartoons, Mickey Mouse, Donald Duck, and Tom and Jerry. We wanted to be like Shirley Temple, we laughed out loud at Laurel and Hardy, but the weekly serial, *Zorro*, was our favourite – we re-enacted his adventures, duelling with imaginary swords and jumping from bed to bed with triumphant cries. On Saturdays, we visited the Hali, the covered market which was more or less in between the main synagogue and the great mosque – very appropriate, since Jews and Muslims had traded there together ever since it had opened in 1909. It looked like a palace from the outside, and inside, with the sun streaming through the windows on the roof and casting magical shadows, the colourful merchandise on the stalls made it the most fascinating of playgrounds. There was a mixture of cultures and scents. Smells of spices, of food – lacerda, the special smoked fish we liked, gooey sweets which we loved, and hot steaming pastries, which we crammed eagerly into our mouths. It was wonderland. Grandmother Rachel and Grandfather Joseph lived close by. We had lunch at their apartment every Saturday: aunts, uncles and all the cousins. We children ran noisily around the big table which was spread over two rooms with the connecting doors open. It was a typical Jewish family occasion. Everyone talked and nobody listened. Everything was discussed from ten different points of views. It was a non-ending debate until Grandmother Rachel sat down and there was peace for a few minutes whilst prayers were said, and then the cacophony began all over again.

Grandfather Joseph was such a kind and quiet man. I can still see him, sipping his tea from the saucer of his cup and holding a cube of sugar in his other hand. He would bite the sugar so delicately before having another sip. He never talked a lot, but his eyes always smiled whenever he saw his grandchildren. We loved him. One day, Stanka, who was back working for us again, picked up Lily and me from school looking very serious, and took us to our grandparents' home. We walked into a dim room. Only the big silver samovar was shining in the corner. Grandfather Joseph was lying on his bed, very pale. His thin aristocratic face was thinner than ever and he did not move. Mama was crying silently and even then I thought how beautiful she was. Apart from the bodies hanging from the trees in the village it was the first time I had seen a dead person. Why did Grandfather have to leave us? They said he had a tumour in his head and it was better that way.

Lily and I began our education at the French School. I was very proud to wear at little hat with a gold metallic *fleur de lis* on the front. I was ambitious and wanted to be the best at everything I did. I had to take great care of Lily on the journeys to and from school, I suppose Papa's methods had paid off, I always knew what tram to catch and when to get off; Lily was often in a dream. But at school, even though she was messy and untidy, she picked up everything very quickly, while I had to slog over it. The lessons were in French which I found difficult to follow even though we spoke a great deal of French at home. I had great problems even though I was attentive and tidy and tried to do everything to make myself a good pupil. I could never understand why I had to work so hard, when some people got it so easy. Nobody had heard of dyslexia then.

Aunt Fanny suggested, very sympathetically, that perhaps I wasn't very bright.

"Don't worry, Annoushka. She will get prettier and marry a rich Jewish man. She'll be a good housewife."

I heard it so many times that I became determined never to marry or be a housewife. Mama was too good-natured to contradict her, but tried to help me as much as she could. On top of that I wasn't developing into the most beautiful girl – as my father would have had me believe. I was stupid and not beautiful, but for sure I wasn't going to give in.

Uncle Hertz used to come regularly to help us with our schooling. I always ended up longest on his lap, while he explained everything patiently to me, again and again; looking at me so kindly above his silver-framed glasses perched on the end of his nose. He never reproached me, no matter how stupid I was. The family used to say that Eleanora had not been lucky with Hertz – 'He speaks twelve languages, but can't earn a penny.' The family were great story tellers. A favourite was that once Hertz had tried to start a business selling eggs. They all arrived broken. I never knew if it were true or not, but in my childish imagination, I pictured all the smashed eggs running out of the truck and it always made me laugh. Uncle Hertz had his difficulties and I had mine.

A smallpox epidemic broke out in Sofia. Many children died but I was the only one in the family to catch it. The apartment was fumigated and I was sent to an isolation ward in the hospital. I remember seeing the shocked faces of Aunt Fanny and Uncle Salomon as I was carried out to the ambulance. Mama remained with me all the time I was in isolation, holding my hand and soothing me.

"Dorchika, you mustn't scratch or you will have scars on your face forever."

I could not stand getting any uglier and that was more than enough to stop me scratching, no matter how terribly I itched. A handsome doctor seemed to be attracted to Mama and paid her a lot of attention. My fear of losing her to him was greater than the discomfort of all the itching and aching, but I had the best treatment because Mama never left my side, and the doctor never seemed to leave her. As soon as he came into the room I purposely began to talk about Papa. There was still no news of him. I don't know how long I was in hospital but it seemed a very long time. I eventually recovered and Mama and I returned to Hardy at Aunt Fanny's apartment.

King Boris's brother, Prince Cyril, who had been appointed Regent, was executed along with many members of the old regime, and Bulgaria was now a Communist country under strict Russian control. Everything had changed. Severe rules were enforced in every aspect of our lives. The Tsar's Square in front of King Boris's palace had been renamed September Square in honour of the revolution, and massive statues of manual workers were erected all around it. On May Day we watched a parade with giant banners depicting Stalin and Lenin and floats promoting the glories of communism and the Soviet Union. One float had a caricature of King Boris begging Hitler on his knees for something or other. Another one had a cruel distortion of Queen Giovanna weeping. The people around me laughed and applauded. I hated it. These were the same people who had wept and lamented when King Boris's funeral procession had passed over this very square. I had been brought up to love our king and believed he had saved us from the Nazis. The entire family were convinced he had been poisoned on the orders of Hitler on his last flight back from Berlin. And it was soon clear that the new authorities no longer liked the Jews either. We were afraid to speak Yiddish or German in the street.

The only person who appeared to have prospered through the entire upheaval was Papa's old friend, Leo. Mama showed us the splendid house where he lived.

"He used to be a poor man, Dora."

We met him once in the street and he told us how

well he was doing under the new regime. Mama's face was expressionless.

Then, all at once, my life was transformed. Papa was alive. A friend of Papa's, who we called Uncle Kostas, had learned through a Jewish network, that Papa was in Vienna, and he wanted us to join him there as soon as possible. We would be a family again. Oh God, it was great. It was wonderful. Everyone was ecstatic. My heart was overflowing with joy and happiness. Nothing bad could ever happen to me again. Papa would take care of us once more. Mama was full of hope for a new life. Uncle Kostas told us that Papa was doing well and lived in the centre of Vienna on top of a building.

"He knows I don't like heights. When we get there he will find somewhere else for us," Mama said confidently.

7

Journey to Vienna

Getting out of Bulgaria was far from easy: passports and papers had to be obtained. Officials had to be bribed and more buttons disappeared from Mama's coat, but after waiting what seemed like forever, permission to leave was given at last. It was all so very, very exciting. The entire family contributed suitcases of various shapes and sizes, in which we crammed our belongings. We had seven suitcases with us when the day finally came and we went to the station to board the train. Everyone was there: Grandmother Rachel, and all the aunts, uncles and cousins. Goodbyes were said and everybody was crying. The rest had no idea what was going to happen to them. They now had hopes of going to Israel, like the vast majority of Bulgarian Jews, but had no idea if they would be allowed to go. We were the lucky ones. We were off to Vienna, to Papa and a better life. I had no regrets in leaving Sofia. I had seen a lot in my nine years. There was nothing there I really liked or would miss. I did not hanker after anything, apart from being with Mama, Papa and Hardy. I was so happy when I boarded that train with my doll in my hand.

The journey to Vienna was painfully long. The train seemed to stop and stand still more than it moved, and when it moved it was agonisingly slow. All Europe remained in utter chaos from the war, millions of displaced persons were swirling around, desperately seeking a home. To make matters worse, the euphoria of victory had all too soon departed and the continent was rapidly being divided into two armed camps. Russian military police got on and off all the time and we feared they would find something wrong with our papers. We kept very quiet, trying not to be noticed. It had become a habit with us. We had had too much misfortune and suffering. It was best to be invisible even in a crowded train. The hard wooden benches in Third Class soon became painful, and Mama looked and was exhausted. We cuddled up to her as close as possible, hardly giving her any room to move. She put her hands on our heads and whispered soothingly in her familiar words.

"Soon it will be better, my *pipihandeles, mouselas, bebbyles*."

We were on that train for what seemed like days and days. The food that we had brought soon ran out and we were frightened, cold and oh – so hungry. On the third day, the door of the wagon opened, there were no compartments, and two Russian soldiers came in. They were ordinary soldiers not like the military police on the train. They looked at us, but we were too exhausted to react. I could feel Mama holding us tighter to her body. They bent over her and began to converse with her in Russian. They had honest peasant faces. Mama relaxed and nodded. One sat next to her, the other opposite. One took Hardy on his lap and the other me, and gave us each a piece of dark bread. It was stale and hard, but tasted wonderful. They then put their rough army greatcoats over us, and we fell asleep. Mama could rest at last and take a nap. There were still good Russians in the world.

We had to disembark at Budapest. When we went to the luggage van several of our suitcases had disappeared. Hardy, trying to be the man, busied himself organising the rest. It was impossible to move money from country to country, so Mama had given money to a Jewish family in Sofia who had a relation, a Rabbi, in Budapest. He should have been there waiting for us to bring us to a safe place with food, and give us new papers to get over the Austrian border. But nobody was there. We stood forlorn while Mama scanned the platform desperately.

"The Rabbi didn't come," I heard her say quietly to herself.

Mama found a small cheap hotel close to the station, and we dragged our luggage to it in relays. Twenty steps and I would sit on the suitcase with my doll, while Hardy and Mama brought up the rest. We repeated this over and over again until all the suitcases arrived at the hotel. We went up to the room exhausted. It smelt mouldy. There was only one weak light bulb and the dimness made it spooky. Heavy faded velvet curtains framed the dirty window. In front of the window was a table with a maroon patterned tablecloth with some rickety chairs around it. There was one double bed covered with a bedspread in another dark pattern. I was used to Mama making everything light and clean. Even in the hut and the ghetto she had made us a home. This was so depressing. And on top of that we were terribly hungry.

Mama gave us a smile, trying to comfort us. She looked exasperated. I could tell that she didn't know what to do next. She pulled aside the bedspread and oh! It was great. There were white, shining sheets, clean pillows and a big soft eiderdown. Hardy and I undressed and climbed into the white cocoon and looked up expectantly at Mama, like two hungry little birds in a nest.

"Go to sleep. When you wake up, food will be here." And she left.

She came back an hour or so later with a piece of salami and one ring less on her finger. It tasted wonderful. I have loved Hungarian salami to this day.

The next morning we began the final leg of the journey to Vienna. We didn't have all the right papers but Mama presented what we had very confidently, with her most charming smile, and we got through. As we neared Papa our emotions played tricks with us. We cried for nothing, laughed without any reason. The tension was mounting so high, it could have reached Mount Blanc. The train eventually arrived at the Hauptbahnhof. My head was hanging out of the window. The platform was full of whirling smoke from the engine. It cleared for a moment and then I saw him, looking anxiously at the train, not knowing if we had finally come back to him.

"Papa!"

I wanted to be first in his arms. The train stopped and I opened the door and ran out of the wagon, but he rushed in by another door. I ran back and saw him holding Mama in his arms. "Papa…Papa! Papa…"

He swept me up and kissed me.

"My little Dorale!"

8

Vienna

Vienna: Summer, 1947. Few of the buildings were standing intact, most were still in ruins. It was a seedy place; one could feel the harshness of surviving in the streets, and could see the distrust in everyone's eyes. Their eyes looked different to the Bulgarians. Bulgarians were rough, but they looked you straight in the eyes. They were not, as Mama would say, refined, but you knew where you stood. The Viennese were different. Their mouths were smiling but their eyes were devious. I had learned to look at eyes from a very early age. Mama's eyes were like a book, full of love. When Hardy or I did something naughty, Papa's eyes were enough to put us in our place. I was lost in Vienna. The people were eyeless. Someone once described Vienna in the years following the war, as an old courtesan dying in a poorhouse, who when the doctor made his rounds, could still shape her cracked lips into the confident smile of a woman whom men had loved. He was right.

Our new home was in the *1st Bezirke*, on the once fashionable Kärnterstrasse, the equivalent of Bond Street in London. But Kärnterstrasse was far from elegant now. It had been among the most destroyed areas in the final liberation of the city. It was mostly a heap of ruins from the gutted Opera House at one end to the roofless Stephan Cathedral at the other. Like Berlin, Vienna had been cut up like a *Sachertorte* into four sectors by the USA, Britain, France and the Soviet Union, but the *1st Bezirke*, the centre of the city, was designated an international zone and the four powers took turns to control it on a monthly basis. Everything that could happen happened in the *1st Bezirke*. It was a dangerous place – especially at night. Women were raped, mostly by the Russian soldiers. People were kidnapped, bundled into cars and never seen again. Displaced young people, without homes or countries, had become feral and lived in the ruins, hunting and thieving in packs. But if you wanted to eat, smoke or wear nylon stockings it was the place to be – and our new home was slap in the middle of it. Policing it was a combined operation, four men in a jeep in different uniforms, just as in *The Third Man*. They hardly did anything – it was all for show. The black market was flourishing, one couldn't get by without it, even the remains of the aristocracy were in it, and it was centred in the *1st Bezirke*. The Western powers usually turned a blind eye, but it was a different matter during the months the Soviets were in control, then the *1st Bezirke* suddenly became very quiet. There was nothing the Russians liked better than to crush burgeoning capitalism and confiscate the goods.

Denazification was still the order of the day and Papa had been allocated a penthouse that had previously belonged to a top Nazi official. It was not very large, consisting of two rooms, plus kitchen and bath. It had been perfect for Papa living on his own, but it was rather small for the four of us. Papa slept on the settee in the sitting room which doubled as his office. He had furnished it himself – a big desk with bookshelves behind it; two round tables on which were strange, exotic ornaments; two comfortable chairs and paintings on the walls. A door led out of Papa's room to the balcony, which stretched the length of the apartment, in front of which was the tin roof of the apartment beneath us. The other room, which we three occupied, had a big wardrobe, two settees, dining table, four chairs, and a large box where the bedclothes were stored during the day. The kitchen was quite comfortable and we would often sit around the little table there, waiting for Papa to return with sugar, chocolate or salami. We were never hungry, but space was indeed tight. Papa liked to have things exactly the way he wanted them and there was little room for us to manoeuvre in, but nothing really mattered – we were together as a family and on our own.

Papa's new business was the black market. You couldn't live in Vienna at that time unless you dealt in it either as a buyer or seller. There was hardly any other business that you could do – especially if the war had robbed you of all that you had had. Many successful businesses in Austria and Germany were founded on the black market at that time. Papa had thrown himself into it with all his customary energy. All types of men were continually coming in and out of Papa's office. Some carried packages in, others carried packages out. You seldom saw the same ones again – always new faces that never stayed long or made conversation. I didn't like them. I would peep in and see the settee, tables and chairs covered with sparkling jewellery, watches, tins of coffee, and piles and piles of money. German Reichmarks, Occupation Schillings and Austrian National Schillings, all tied separately in neat bundles. Three currencies, but no one really trusted cash. The most powerful currency was cigarettes, especially American cigarettes: Chesterfields and Lucky Strikes. A suitcase full of Chesterfields would buy you a lorry, and Papa had carton after carton of them stacked all around the room. But cigarettes didn't interest me. I would creep in sometimes when Papa was out, and touch the ornaments and imagine the distant lands they had come from – China, Japan – and see coloured silk robes and cherry blossom.

But we didn't go back to our old life. My eyes opened all too quickly. Papa had changed. He was so much thinner and on his passport photo, which had been taken the previous year, he looked like a skeleton. He never spoke about it in front of me, but Hardy discovered many years later, that he had been sent Banjica, the most notorious concentration camp in all of Yugoslavia. It was a punishment camp, not a death camp like Auschwitz, but its inmates, partisans and anti-fascists as well as Jews, suffered far longer. Papa was there for almost a year and I have no idea how he survived. Before arriving at the camp the prisoners were beaten and tortured by the Gestapo for several days. The Commandant, Svetozar Vujkovic, a pro-Nazi Serb, was a psychopath who took delight in shooting prisoners, including children, at random. On one occasion he personally shot twenty young girls. Nearly 4000 inmates either died of starvation or were executed in mobile gas vans. In the autumn of 1944, knowing they were losing the war, the Nazis began to make frantic efforts to hide their atrocities. Paul Babel, who had directed the massacre at Babi Yar, where over 30,000 Jews, almost the entire Jewish population of Kiev were butchered, came to Banjica and personally oversaw the disinterment and burning of bodies, by chain gangs of the surviving Serb and Jewish prisoners. Papa had endured and lived through all that, and had then survived a death march before he had been finally freed. He had never been a religious man but I don't think he ever set foot in a synagogue after the war. He had lost his faith in any God who could allow such things as he had seen. He went out practically every evening and came back late, usually when I was asleep. He was desperate for life, knowing how quickly it could end.

Mama no longer went with him but stayed in with us. She didn't like Vienna at all. She came from Russia, had been brought up in quiet Varna, and had had a beautiful ordered life in Sofia before the war. The *1st Bezirke* was full of whores, thieves and black marketeers – people who took what they could and didn't care who they hurt in the process. Moreover she was lonely. She missed her sisters and her close-knit family. She gave us all her love but cried quietly on her own. I understood little, if anything, of what was going on.

I had grown out of my clothes, my doll was now

wearing one of my dresses, and it was almost impossible to buy new ones, even on the black market. Papa brought home some brightly coloured flags and Mama endeavoured to make me dresses out of them. They were very pretty, but the rough material itched dreadfully and I couldn't wear them.

Sometimes I would walk with Papa in the streets. He seemed to know everyone. When we passed the taxi drivers waiting in the nearby Neue Markt, they would all cry out:

"*Servus, Emil! Wie gets*?"

He acknowledged and replied to every one of them.

"Do you really know all these people Papa? Why do you speak to them? They are only drivers"

"Dora, never be too proud. Greet everybody equally with respect. You never know when you will be down."

Why did I have to think of down? We were up! We had been down enough.

He would pop into *gasthauses* and bars, do a tour of the tables, meet people, discuss business or have a drink. I was not allowed in and waited outside. I was shy but very curious, and my eyes missed nothing. Sometimes he talked to women who had heavy paint on their faces. Their hair was too coiffured and I thought they showed too much of their legs. Papa seemed to enjoy their company. He teased them and laughed with them. I didn't like it, but he would come out and put his hand on my shoulder and we would go on our way as if nothing had happened. I always liked it best when we went along the Graben to Demel's *Kaffee-Konditorei* by the Hofburg, where white-aproned waitresses would serve us their version of the *Sachertorte*, a delicious chocolate cake filled with apricot. In those elegant surroundings, which had been spared the bombing, it was easy to forget the devastation and sordidness outside and all our misery of the past years. Papa and I would chat away and I felt as close to him as I had ever been. But there were other days when he was distant, unreachable, enclosed within himself.

Nevertheless he was always exciting. Things were never boring when he was around. One morning, very early, there was a terrifying noise – as if bombs were falling all over again on the tin roof outside. I peeped through the curtain and all I saw were boots and the bottom of brown army coats. It was the Russians. It was obviously their turn to be in charge of the *1st Bezirke*. But what were they doing on the tin roof? They all poured through the door into Papa's room. We heard lots of orders, questions, the opening and banging of drawers and cupboards. We were terrified and hid under the table, thinking that they were coming to pick us up. We stayed there until we heard them leave. Papa had been taken again. His room was a shambles. The Russians had left with their pockets filled – there was no trace of the goods and money that had been there the day before. Contrary to our fears, Papa worked his usual magic and came back the next day, but without his watches, jewellery, cigarettes and cash.

Mama was in constant touch with the family in Sofia, who like the vast majority of Bulgarian Jews were preparing to immigrate to Israel. They had been granted permission at last. They wrote happy letters, looking forward to a new and better life, believing that their luck was finally changing. But their suffering was not quite complete: a few weeks before they departed, Lily, impetuous as ever, jumped off a tram too early, slipped and lost a leg when she was run over by the wheel. Mama cried at the news; so did I. They all left for Israel nevertheless.

"Dorchika, you have to go to school."

Our education so far had been sadly lacking. Hardy had been sent to the Theresianum, the most prestigious boarding school in Vienna, founded by the Empress Maria Theresa herself. A school had to be found for me that would take a girl that spoke a little French, Bulgarian and Yiddish, but hardly a word of German, and I was sent to the nearest, a convent school in Johannesgasse, two streets down the Kärnterstrasse, almost next door to the Vienna Conservatorium. Every day I passed I could hear the sounds of different musical instruments floating out of the windows. There I was, a Jewish girl surrounded by nuns, praying after every lesson and going to church services in the nearby Annakirche every evening before I went home. I am sure my parents had no idea of the whole procedure and what it was all about, and I didn't tell them. The other girls were polite, clean and properly dressed. It was so different from the French school in Sofia, where the children came from different walks of life. It was a convent with Jesuit influences and I soon began to be brainwashed. I liked the quietness and peace of the Annakirche, with its beautiful painted ceiling, the priests in their theatrical robes, the nuns with their starched headgear, like great white butterflies, and the shining rosaries hanging from their waists, which they continually fondled as they taught their lessons. I especially liked Sister Theresa, who looked straight into my eyes as she talked to me so quietly – patiently explaining everything for hours and hours on end.

"Who is God?"

"Where is he?"

"Why doesn't he do something to bring Mama and Papa together again? They are together but not together."

"Why did he make the war and spoil my life?"

"Why did he make us wear yellow stars?"

I went on and on.

She would bend her white butterfly wings down to me and talk and talk and talk. I listened intently, but what impressed me most were her soft blue eyes and her little red cheeks and the goodness that seemed to shine out of her. I still see her face in front of me. The longer I spent there, the more I became attracted with the mystique. In the lunch hour I would go into the little chapel and sit on my own. I had watched the communion services with the girls all in white with their hair crowned with flowers. Eventually, I decided that it was time for me to convert, and Sister Theresa was delighted when I told her that I also wanted to take communion in a white dress with flowers in my hair.

But when I told Mama my intention she took me out of that school the very next day.

Home was no longer the same. My father now had a secretary, who came every day. When I got back from school she was still at the apartment, with him in his office. I felt uncomfortable with her being there and I could see that Mama didn't like her either. I hated the tension and the continual little flare-ups. Hardy used to come home every second weekend, and Mama was so happy to see him that she practically ignored me on those occasions. Naturally I became jealous. Hardy and I quarrelled constantly, he ordered me about more than ever, and the end result was always a fight and I usually ended up with bruises all over. But I preferred it when he was there, I didn't have to face the tension alone. At least I could fight with him or go with him to the cinema. Papa continued to take me out occasionally, and when he did he always chose the most elegant and chicest places; Hotel Sacher was his particular favourite. It was the grandest hotel in Vienna and had been comparatively untouched by the bombing. It had been the British headquarters during the early part of the occupation and every visiting dignitary or celebrity stayed there. Café Sacher was famous for its own version of *Sachertorte* and *Kaffee mit Schlag*, but Papa always chose the Red Bar. It wasn't a bar at all but the most beautiful restaurant, the walls, ceiling, and lushly upholstered couches, all covered with scarlet damask. It had huge crystal chandeliers and the crispest, whitest tablecloths, and a multitude of paintings. It was an art gallery in itself. The *maître d'* was yet another friend of Papa's, and he always had my favourite dish *Tafelspitzer* (boiled beef and horseradish), specially prepared for me. But such treats became more and more infrequent.

In December 1947 the new Austrian Schilling was introduced overnight. Papa had just sold a vast stock of American cigarettes and had been paid in the old currency, which was virtually worthless. We were down again, but not for long. Papa knew how to work the black market. He had so many contacts. If Harry Lime had existed, Papa would have known him.

9

I Want To Dance

"Mama, I want to dance and dance. I want to be a ballerina. Please, Mama! Please Papa! Please! Please!"

"Doralie, you move very nicely, but a Jewish girl dancing on the stage is not for our family."

And the subject was closed again and again and again. But I persisted. One day I approached my father at exactly the right moment and I finally succeeded. Mother fell in behind him, and I was taken to the Opera School for the entry examination. The Opera House had been destroyed and the school was in a cellar of the Theater-an-der-Wein, where Beethoven's *Fidelio* had been first performed in 1805. I was full of confidence when we entered the grand old theatre and went down the stairs to a big room containing only a few mirrors and a dance bar. There were a lot of little girls and I seemed to be the oldest. All the others were small and delicate, with everything in the right proportion. I appeared to be the wrong shape: my body was much too short to accommodate my long legs and neck. Mama had pulled my hair tight at the back, in proper ballerina style, but bits stuck out everywhere. Barefooted in gymslip and pants, I stood, holding on to the bar, awaiting instructions. They came but I didn't understand them. They sounded like mumbo-jumbo.

Everyone else knew what to do and I tried desperately to copy them. I could feel how awkward I was. The only movement instructions I had ever received was my mother teaching me how to curtsey to the elders.

My eyes were wide with anger as I stared at the ballet mistress. Why was she doing this to me? It had taken me years to persuade my parents, and now she wasn't even giving me a chance. Her peroxided blonde hair was as unreal as the sounds that came from her mouth. After she had made her choice of those who would join the Grand Opera Ballet School, she came to me and guided me to the bar.

"Pick up your leg."

I did.

"And in the back please."

I did.

"Go and change. I will have a word with your mother."

Mother joined me after a while and we walked out of that dreadful cellar that had all but suffocated my dream of becoming a ballerina.

"*Mousela! Peppihandler!*" She used her own endearing play words when she wanted to dampen the blows. "You are too old, Doralie. They only take children under eight years old, and then they must have had previous training at another ballet school. Your muscles are too stiff now."

It was so unfair. How could I have had previous training in the hut or the ghetto?

She kissed me so lovingly. That night I cuddled close to her and cried myself to sleep.

I think in a way my parents were relieved. Although it was nice to go to the theatre, it was not for their daughter. But I had been dreaming for so long, I wasn't going to give up my dream now.

10

Boarding School in Hietzing

It was decided it was best for me to go to a boarding school: the Metzger Pensionat in the wealthy district of Hietzing, on the edge of the Vienna Woods. Boarding schools for girls were rare; indeed, it was the only one of its type in all Austria; the pupils were mostly children of ambassadors, wealthy actors or rich divorcees. The school was in a fine-looking mansion opposite the Schönbrunn Palace with large and beautiful gardens.

I was assigned to a dormitory with fourteen beds, all neatly made up. There was a big piano for music practice during the day. Individual cupboards for clothes were in the corridor and a food cabinet was on the floor below, where we kept our special treats in individual boxes. We were only allowed to open the boxes when the mistress opened the cupboard. This usually happened after dinner, and there was much hustle and bustle as we exchanged goodies with one another. Everybody looked forward to that time as we were often hungry. The dining room consisted of two long, long tables, which different pupils were assigned to lay out every day in a correct and exact manner, as if we were going to enjoy a delicious five-course meal. On the contrary, the food was mostly inedible. I hated porridge soup most.

"Porridge soup again!" My stomach would get cramps just thinking about it. We all got exactly equal portions poured onto our plates by the surly kitchen staff, who considered us all to be spoilt little rich girls, and enjoyed watching us suffer with their uneatable menu. I remembered Papa's advice and tried to be nice to them in the hope of receiving a smaller portion, but they were unmoveable. The sitting arrangements were irregular, but I always tried to be far away from the head of the table, which was occupied by our housemistress. I had figured a way of how to dispose of the dreaded porridge soup. I would guide my spoon towards my mouth and then quickly drop it into the water glass, which I was balancing between my legs beneath the table. I would then excuse myself and as gracefully as I could, hiding the glass in front of me, disappear into the toilette.

My father had given me free rein to supplement my diet by ordering anything I wanted from the nearby stores. I did not always choose the healthiest things. Pralines were my favourites. They were in lots of different colours and I would order them by the box. Little secret nightly feasts were organised. We were all very individual and different. Unlike the convent, religion didn't matter and was never discussed. The rumour was that the mansion had been the home of Kaiser Franz Joseph's mistress, and there was a secret passage to his palace, so that they could visit each other secretly and have wild nights. Although we were not sure what wild nights meant, we made great efforts to find the tunnel, but it never emerged.

I had developed a sense of style very early. When Mama came to pick me up in a chauffeur-driven car or attended parents' meetings, I always told her what to wear. Shoes, handbag, gloves, hat with a big veil – everything she wore, from top to bottom in the same tone. Pale grey suited her best. I was so proud of her. She was as elegant and beautiful as any actress or ambassador's wife. I enjoyed the school but missed Mama terribly. I was allowed to go to the Directress's office and phone her when it got unbearable. The Directress was tall with black hair and brown eyes and a big sympathetic smile. One day after a particularly tearful call, she tried to take my mind off my troubles.

"Dora, what do you want to be in the future?"

"Ballerina."

She smiled and laid her hand on my shoulder, "Don't you think it is time we started doing something about it?"

I had always liked her, but now she was definitely my favourite, and I promised myself that when I was grown up and beautiful, I would marry her son. He was only ten years older than me and was desired by every girl in the school. I did well there. I enjoyed maths, chemistry and sports. Needlepoint still bored me. My reading was slow, I found the words difficult, but I enjoyed reading. My best friend, Christel, introduced me to Karl May's exciting Cowboy and Indian stories and I began to read them under my blanket by torchlight.

Once a week we had a big bath day. Six girls went into the bathroom at a time. It was full of steam.

We had to scrub ourselves and wash our hair before being thoroughly examined for cleanliness by the housemistress. Her little eyes would peer out of her glasses as she looked behind our ears and into our hair, sending all who failed her inspection back into the steaming bath. She was like a little virginal bird – short, shrilling voice, black, short-cropped hair and skin from which colour had been drained, even from her lips which rarely smiled. Her steps were quick and so were her hands if she caught us talking during the prep hours.

It was difficult to control a bunch of embryonic young ladies, full of high spirits and imagination, doing anything that would defy the rules. We were kept in by iron gates and nobody was allowed out except under supervision. There was a large cross fixed on the outside wall. We discovered that if we climbed from the balcony of our room, we could step onto the cross and then slide down slowly to freedom. That cross became very useful. We made several successful escapes from our comfortable prison. We went to the centre of Hietzing, pretending to be grown-ups at ten years old. We sat in the coffee house drinking coffee, eating chocolates and giggling a lot about nothing in particular. We were of course eventually found out by the housemistress and strongly reprimanded

My parents had separated. Mama moved into Favoritenstrasse. She rented two rooms in an old lady's apartment opposite the Theresianum so that Hardy could visit her more frequently. Mama never complained, but she looked very unhappy. She didn't sing and laugh as she used to, but she still cuddled me a lot and held me tightly to her breast whenever I came home to her. I was constantly busy and had no patience – there was so much to do: rearranging my room, talking to our old landlady, walking her small schnauzer dog, doing her shopping, or taking a tram to meet my best friend, Christel. Christel's mother was an actress, and I always thought her to be a little bit mad, but I liked her father, who was our family doctor and one of Papa's many friends. Dr Sponberger was a tall, kindly man who had lost a leg during the war. I could see their home clearly from the balcony of the apartment in Kärnterstrasse, since all the houses in between had been destroyed. On the way to one of my visits to Christel, I decided to drop in and see my father. I let myself in to the apartment, walked down the corridor and opened the door of what used to be our little room. Papa was in bed with his secretary. I said nothing but ran out and hurtled down the six flights of stairs. I didn't understand. Anger piled up in my heart. I could have killed that woman. How dare she do this to our family? The pain was terrible. I cried and cried, walking nowhere. I couldn't understand how Mama could accept it. She was his wife. Nobody else was. I tried to put it far back in my head and resolved never to open my mouth about it. I didn't go to Christel that weekend. I stayed in my room alone, trying to understand what was happening to my world.

I continued my ordered and regulated life at the boarding school, where we continued to be groomed into becoming sophisticated and cultured young ladies. There were outings to the Vienna Philharmonic, performances of Goethe and Schiller at the Ronacher – temporary home of the still bomb-damaged Burgtheater. I saw my first opera, *Cavalieri Rusticana* – but I was bored and restless and unhappy, until one afternoon I was called into the Directress's office.

"I have made some enquiries. Go and get your coat. We are going into town to take you to a ballet school."

My dream had come true after all.

The Dia Luca School was on the top floor of a well preserved building. It even had a lift. I liked it the moment I walked in: little cubicles left and right along a corridor and at the end, behind a frosted glass door, the ballet room itself. The first cubicle was a small office, where the students paid for the classes. Then they went into the other cubicles to change before they entered the ballet room. It was kept meticulously clean. At one end was an enormous mirror and at the other, a piano and a chair, where Dia Luca herself would sit.

We prepared ourselves before she entered the class and the chatter sounded like chickens in hutches, but as soon as her silhouette, sharp profile with crop hair, became visible behind the glass door, silence fell upon us. Dia Luca was of the old Russian school, with all the power and dignity of a *Grande Dame*. She always had a cigarette in a long holder in her right hand, with which she would point at us individually as she kept us ruthlessly at the bar. She was very strict and never talked except to correct us in her deep voice. She was magic. I fell in love with her and gave her all my childlike devotion. The studio had a glass roof and the sun poured in unmercifully in the summer, the others would complain, but nothing ever disturbed me. I had achieved my dream. But I was bad. My body wasn't limp, my muscles didn't stretch, my legs were long and were difficult to hold up, and my instep went in the opposite direction so that I could never get up on my points. My place was in the last row. Annamarie and Susy were the best pupils. They were fabulous. They were right in the centre of the front row and nobody could hope to move them away from there.

I was taken to the ballet school twice a week and managed to get there early enough to do two classes. I loved everything, even though everything seemed to hurt me. I was stubborn and just got on with it.

Israel had been recognised as a state, and Hardy and I became members of a Zionist Youth movement, the Gordonia-Maccabi Hatzair. The Hashomer were too rough and the Mizrachi too religious. Summer holidays came and we were sent to a camp which Rothschild had provided for the immigrant Jewish children. We thought Rothschild must have been a wonderful man to give this palace and the enormous park, which seemed to stretch forever, to the Jewish community. It was great fun. The girls slept in a great hall, which had once been a grand ballroom, with broken gilt-framed mirrors and faded frescoes. Every morning there was an early call to wash, dress and go on parade, where the blue and white flag of Israel was raised and we sang the *Hatikvah*:

"As long as the Jewish spirit is yearning deep in the heart,
With eyes turned towards the East, looking towards Zion,
Then our hope, the two thousand-year hope, will not be lost,
To be a free people again, in our land, the land of Zion and
Jerusalem."

Our eyes filled with tears as we sang and looked on the flag. No one spoke of their past. We were living for now.

We were trained for life on a kibbutz. We had to go on night watch, which scared me. I was always freezing cold. The Hashomer had a camp not far from us, and for some reason we were in constant war with each other. We stayed up all night, guarding our flag. I was never sure why – it was exactly the same as their flag. On other occasions we were taken into the middle of a field and had to find our way back. Sometimes we slept in tents and as I was the youngest, I didn't understand what all the giggling was about. I was cold, wet and uncomfortable. To eat from a tin plate in front of the campfire was not my idea of fun either. But I loved the sporting activities. I won every sprint race I entered. I couldn't stand losing and pulled out of the competition if I felt I didn't have a good chance.

Kurtie, our group leader, who had been active in the Haganah during the struggle for independence, taught us about the land of Israel. He also told us horrendous stories of what is now known as the Holocaust. The Bulgarian Jews had indeed been lucky. My parents had never talked about the war but I learnt all about it that summer. Auschwitz, Buchenwald, Dachau...

gas chambers...tortures...millions of Jews dead. It was more horrible than anything I had ever imagined. My heart screamed. And my poor father had survived all that. Why did they hate us so much? Kurtie's words were imprinted in my mind forever:

"What happened to the Jewish people in the years of Hitler must never be repeated. We will never allow ourselves to be led again like cattle into the slaughterhouse. We will fight for our freedom and Israel, our own country. No passiveness will come from our generation, or from any generations to come."

My enthusiasm for Israel was inexhaustible, but before I went I wanted to find out about the ballet schools there.

Back in Vienna, the summer holidays continued. Hardy had three special friends, Bummi from Rumania, Peter from Hungary and Tommy from Czechoslovakia. They had all survived the Holocaust one way or another, and were now living life with the greatest enthusiasm. They were great fun and everybody liked them, including Mama. Whenever they called for Hardy, she insisted on giving them some of her famous chicken soup. They were very willing and helpful. They carried and humped and delivered and did any small job they could find to earn a little extra money, and they knew certain places where they were always very welcome. Sometimes they would take me along with them to a Hungarian Restaurant. The owner would let us go into the front room, where patrons would wait to be seated. There was a big round table at which we would sit and share a huge bowl of goulash with bread galore. It was a feast – and all for free.

Holidays finished at last and it was back to boarding school. I was promoted to a smaller dormitory with only six beds, but I was still the youngest. There was blonde Eva, black-haired Helga with flashing eyes, and constantly smiling Ingrid – they were a bunch of unusually beautiful girls, and I was in great awe of everything they did. I listened in bed at night as they spoke about sex and boys.

"Open your legs and put a piece of rolled up paper between your thighs."

They all did.

"Squeeze hard."

I couldn't understand the point of it all, and retreated under the blanket with my cowboy book. I found it much more exciting.

A ball was arranged for the senior girls and boys from a nearby school were invited. I crept out with Christel, who had remained in the other dormitory, and stood at the top of the winding stairs, looking down at the older girls passing by in their mothers' pre-war ball gowns. I thought they were beautiful and I couldn't wait to be old enough to join them. Christel soon found it very boring and couldn't wait to get back Karl May. I wanted to stay. Christel won. We heard the quick little steps of our housemistress and we had to retreat into our rooms.

A few days later I was summoned again to the Directress's office.

"Dora, I've called you down to let you know that your fees have not been paid for several months. Since I have to pay the bills at the store from which you have purchased considerable amounts of Pralines, I would appreciate it if you could moderate it somehow."

What can be wrong now? The last time I had seen Papa he had introduced me to Baroness Esterhazy. She was very elegant with a silver fox over her shoulder and very friendly towards me. I didn't sense any money troubles but in my family you didn't talk about such things.

"And my ballet?" I asked.

"You will continue as usual. I will take care of it until the end of the year. I hear you are making good progress."

At least that was secured.

Shortly afterwards I was accused of stealing goodies from the food cupboard. A meeting was called and I was confronted by the housemistress, who had always disliked me. My fervent denials were to no avail. In her eyes I was the obvious choice. Christel was the only one who thought it was all too stupid for words, and retreated into her books. I was badly hurt. Boarding school didn't seem to be the same anymore.

"Dora, will you go to the office. Your mother is here."

I ran quickly down. Strange – there was never a visit in the middle of the week. Mama looked very sad and dignified. She wasn't dressed in her usual elegant style.

She wore a brown coat and hat. She knew I didn't like that colour. Why did she wear it? I kissed her hand as I had been taught to do in public. She took me close to her and smiled. I sensed the warmth, love and compassion floating towards me. She spoke very quietly.

"Dorchika, I will come and pick you up at the end of the week. Please pack all your things – you are coming home."

There were no questions on my part. I could guess why – the bills.

She kissed me and left. I turned to the Directress. "Mama is always dressed as a lady. Something must be wrong," was all that I could say.

"Dora, your mother will always be a lady. Clothes have nothing to do with it."

She was so clever and kind. She brought up young ladies, and I had behaved like a stupid, superficial little girl. I went up to the dormitory and cried. Thank God, it was revision time and nobody could see me.

11

First Steps

Mama came to pick me up as arranged and took me home. But home was now Kärnterstrasse once more. Did that mean that Mama and Papa were back together? Hardy had also been taken out of the Theresianum, and we did everything we could to push them together again. We even behaved. I had to change schools in the middle of the year. I went from my pampered little private school for young ladies, to an enormous mixed institution run by the State. It was a drastic change. The boys, and some of the girls, were noisy and rough, there was a lot of pushing and bullying. I became shyer and shyer and retreated into myself. I fell back with my studies. The lessons were agony. I couldn't follow them, I had been taught in so many different languages. Everyone spoke in the sing-song Viennese dialect which I found hard to understand. I spoke Papa's pure *Hochdeutsch*. My dictation was a disaster – I just couldn't do it. I was lucky to get five words right on a page. Maths came easier, but if I had to stand up in class and explain a theory or problem, my mouth couldn't keep up with the speed of my brain and the words I uttered were pure mumbo jumbo. But I had imagination. At the end of the year there was a class competition for the most entertaining little play.

I conceived a plot and persuaded two girls, Helga and Mitzi, to be in it with me. I acted a comedy part and discovered that I could be funny and liked telling people what to do. I had found a way to escape my shyness, and we won the competition.

I took no interest in boys, they bored me, but I grew fond of Helga and Mitzi, and we always walked home from school together. Mitzi's father was a concierge, a very low-paid job, but I remembered my father's advice and was always very nice to her. Nevertheless, I preferred Helga, who lived close by. Her parents ran an embroidery business from their flat. There was a workroom full of imitation pearls, beads and sequins. Helga's father delivered the embroidery at the end of the day, and Helga and I would hurry from school to make sure we had a peep at the latest creations before they left the flat. Then, when the workers had gone home, we would go into their room and pick up whatever had fallen on the floor. To us, they were precious jewels from which we could make earrings and necklaces. We looked at ourselves in the mirror, dressed in our plain school outfits with gaudy earrings hanging from our ears and sparkling glitter around our necks, and imagined we looked beautiful and so grown-up. But I had no desire to look older. I knew too well that I was really too old to become a ballerina.

Helga had short thick black hair. She was quite small like me but was very vivacious, and being an only child, was quite spoilt. She had two great passions – the cinema and patisserie shops, which suited me very well. In winter, we spent most of our weekends around such establishments. In summer, we would often go with her parents to their little garden outside the city. We would go there by tram and take a basket loaded with food. Helga and her mother would wear dirndls, the traditional Austrian dress, with floral embroidered bodice and white blouse with fluffy sleeves, whilst her father would wear lederhosen and Tyrolean hat – as if they were going up into the mountains instead of the suburbs. The little garden had a hut with wooden chairs and a table, plates – everything you needed for a perfect picnic. Papa could never understand the point of picnics. "Are there no restaurants?" he used to ask, but I always looked forward to going. That is, until one day when Helga's father asked me to sit on his lap. Helga was picking flowers and her mother was nowhere to be seen. Helga's father was wearing his short lederhosen; his bare hairy knees rubbed against me and itched. He held me tight and something happened. I didn't know what it was, but made me feel very uncomfortable. I twisted away from him and kept my distance from then on. But one afternoon, I went round to Helga's flat so that we could do our homework together. Her father opened the door and invited me in. He told me Helga was out but would be back soon. My heart sank when he asked me to sit next to him on the sofa. I wouldn't sit down and chatted nonstop, and was very relieved when Helga appeared. I didn't visit Helga so frequently after that.

Mitzi was plump with blonde plaits hanging down her back. I didn't like visiting her home either. It consisted of a small room on the ground floor where you could hear everybody coming in or going out – I couldn't understand how anyone could get a moment's peace to sleep there. It was crammed with furniture, so that it was difficult to move around without bumping into something. It also had a stale, lingering smell. In my orderly mind cleanliness and tidiness were imperative. But I liked Mitzi, or perhaps, I used her. She would help me with any problems I had with my homework, and I relied on her when there were any tests or exams. I would manage to sit next to her and she became a busy beaver, doing her work as well as mine. I made quite a study of learning how to cheat. It would have been logical of course to revise for exams, but I had answers written over all parts of my body. The problem was remembering which part responded to which answer. Should I look at my knee before my arm or my arm before my knee? I failed everything except maths, chemistry and music. My interest and concentration were on only one thing – the ballet.

I still attended Dia Luca's classes even though the boarding school had stopped paying for them. I trained scrupulously, hoping that I would get to the front row, between Susy and Annemarie. But they were still there and I was still at the back. I worked even harder. I worked when everyone else rested between bar and floor exercises. I never seemed to get tired. I had blisters on my toes, but it was a small price to pay if I could only get into the front row. I could feel I was getting better; there was nothing for me but the top.

Though my parents were now back living in the same apartment, they didn't seem to be together. Something was missing. My father was as always larger than life, my mother ever more quiet and reserved. I was close to my father during the day, but at night I always cuddled up to Mama. Hardy was usually out with his friends, wheeling and dealing or chasing girls. Papa was no longer making a fortune; the black market had become much more difficult. Things began to disappear out of the apartment – ornaments, paintings. Mama didn't have her fur coat. She made furtive visits to the Dorotheum at the bottom of Kärnterstrasse, where hard-up members of the middle class had pawned their goods since 1707. The food was not so good either. It was even difficult to find the money for Dia Luca's classes. On one occasion, bailiffs came and stuck labels on the furniture, which I pulled off the moment they had gone. My father often came home a little drunk. I tried not to see it, and of course we didn't talk about such things. But I was shocked to see him in that state. He had always been so meticulous about his appearance, his ties and shirts were changed daily to match the colour of his suit, a silk handkerchief was always in his top pocket, a white silk scarf around his neck, his shoes were polished every day – in the winter he even wore spats to protect them. Shoes were one of his great passions. He must have had fifty pairs: black, brown and two-toned, complete with wooden shoe-trees. He still wore his green jacket with the velvet collar every morning, but his smile was sad.

One day, Dia Luca asked my parents if they would

allow me to work in a theatre, which needed children for a simple dance in an operetta they were about to put on. The famous Austrian composer, Robert Stolz, had returned from his enforced exile in Hollywood, where he had received two Oscar nominations, with his latest work, *Springtime in the Prater*. It was a big event, the talk of the town. The Stadttheater was quite close to our home and to my delight my parents agreed. Annemarie and Susy had also been chosen of course. Every evening, I felt quite grown-up as I walked past the still roofless Stephan Cathedral with the finials and gables looking miserable and black against the sky, and across Stephansplatz and over the busy Ring. The other children were taken by their mothers, but I knew Mama would be uncomfortable sitting with them all evening, and always went alone. I had developed my independence very early. There were two performances on Saturday and Sunday, I couldn't get back home, so Mama used to pack me two large French loaves, filled with salami and pickled cucumber, together with a flask of sweet tea.

Annemarie and Susy were amazed. "Dora, where to you put all that?"

But I was always hungry, and couldn't understand how anyone could have the slightest worries with their weight. *Springtime in the Prater,* containing the famous Viennese song, '*Im Prater bluh'n wieder die Baume*', was a huge success and ran for several months, and for a while my classes were paid for without worries.

One afternoon I was in my father's room, looking at some magazines, when Hardy walked in.

"Papa, I am leaving school. I am going to find a job."

"Hardy, you won't. You will continue your education and go to university."

"You can't afford to get me through school and I want to earn my own money."

He was already earning money I thought, buying and selling and playing cards, which he was not supposed to do. The discussion went backwards and forwards. Neither wanted to give in, before finally a compromise was made: Hardy would go to a business school in the evenings and some afternoons, but would be free during the rest of the day to take a job. He got a job in a shoe shop. On his first pay day he came home with three pink *Punschkrapfen*, filled with jam, rum and chocolate, my favourite patisserie, and presented one to each of us. He was always generous. His family came first.

Our family's fortunes were down, but Vienna's were on the way up. Despite being among the most fervent supporters of their fellow countryman, Adolf Hitler – over half a million had been members of the Nazi Party and over a million had served in the Wehrmacht – the Austrians had persuaded the Allies that they had been victims of the Nazis, and they were now receiving masses of aid. Houses were being rebuilt all over the city. The shops had plenty of food again. Well-dressed people were to be found on the streets and in the coffee houses. The Opera House remained a ruin, the Burgtheater was still closed, but the other theatres and cinemas had re-opened and were always full. That winter, Hardy took me to stay at a Jewish club in Simmering for the winter sports. I refused to ski or skate or do anything which could injure my legs and handicap me for ballet. I not only didn't do any sport but I was even petrified to walk on ice or snow in case I fell. I only felt safe inside the grand hotels. Of course we were not residents, but Hardy had friends there with wealthy parents, who could afford to stay in such places. We used to meet them at the luxurious Panhans Hotel. Their girlfriends, who were naturally older than me, ordered any patisserie they wanted, which for me was the height of luxury. It never occurred to them to offer one to me or even give me a taste. I played little games with myself and pretended that I didn't like patisserie. I didn't like the girls much either, they seemed very spoilt and arrogant. Their conversation bored me; they only seemed concerned about boyfriends, marriage, their precious clothes, where they would go on their next holiday, or which bar in Vienna was the in-place to go. They thought they were so worldly and sophisticated, but I knew I had better taste than any of them. The cheap outfits I put together looked just as good as all their expensive clothes.

After a few days, Hardy went off with some of his friends in a car, but I took the train to Vienna. I couldn't wait to get back home. I rang the bell of the apartment and a strange man opened the door.

"Oh, hello." I tried to pass him, thinking he was one of Papa's black marketeers.

He grabbed my arm. "Where do you think you're going?"

"What do you mean? This is my home. I live here. Where are my mother and father?"

"They don't live here anymore. This is my home."

He pushed me out and slammed the door in my face. I stared at the door. Had I made a mistake? It was the top floor. There were three doors. Ours was the last, but there was a different name on the bell. I rang it again but nobody answered. I went back to the lift and checked the floor again. I was right – it was the top. Was I going mad? Had I lost my memory? Had they deserted me? Perhaps the Gestapo were back and they had been picked up. Mama had always told us "Never say you are a Jew." I grew cold and stiff. The blood stopped running through my veins. I rang the neighbour's bell: again no answer. I ran down to the first floor. The concierge was not at home. Back up to the top floor and I pressed the bell of our apartment once again. I heard unfamiliar steps coming down the corridor. The peephole opened and closed but the door did not move. I ran down the stairs and into the street. Everything was as it usually was. It wasn't wartime anymore. Oh, my God, where are Mama and Papa? I stood in busy Kärnterstrasse with tears running down my face. People didn't seem to notice me as they passed. Whatever was I going to do? Then I remembered that Hardy's friend, Tommy, lived close by. I ran to his flat. I had never been inside it. His father was an artist who had survived Buchenwald and wasn't well. He hardly ever came out and spent nearly all his time painting. Tommy opened the door.

"Tommy, where are my parents?" I could hardly speak. My voice was cracking as I tried to hold back my tears.

"Come in, Dora."

I couldn't believe what I saw. All along the walls were paintings of people looking like skeletons, hanging on barbed wire, with holes as eyes, yellow and blue, which pierced right through me. Strangely, those terrible paintings calmed me down. I followed Tommy into the kitchen.

"Sit down, Dora." He gave me a cup of tea. "Your flat belonged to a Nazi, and they have given it back to him. The Nazis are getting everything back. Your parents were thrown out. They had to leave within the day."

I didn't understand it. "Are they alright? Where are they? I knocked on every neighbour's door but they didn't answer. Is it because I am a Jew?"

"They have taken some rooms in the 2nd *Bezirke*. I have the address. They are waiting there for you."

I left my little suitcase with Tommy and ran all the way, across the temporary footbridge over the Danube, to the *2nd Bezirke*. I knew it was a bad area, and when I saw the house my fears were confirmed. They were in a flat on the 1st floor. Mama opened the door.

"Oh, Mama! Mama!"

"Dorchika! Mousela! "

She held me in her arms as her loving words swept over me and at that moment the world ceased to exist. As always, she was trying to shield me from the horrors and everything that could hurt me. My only real home was in her arms.

I went into a meagre little room. Our dining table and chairs were there, a bed and a wardrobe.

"Hungry, Dorchika?"

"Starving."

I sat at the table and she brought me sweet tea and piece of white bread. There was no salami, but I savoured it.

"Dorchika, we have lost everything. But there is nothing very much to worry about. Papa will take care of us. We are sharing this flat with some Greeks, but it won't be very long before we move." She made it sound so simple and easy. She was so small and delicate. How could she take it all?

Papa arrived soon after full of life, as if nothing had happened. "Dorale, I could drop you off in the middle of the desert and you will find your way out."

"But Papa, I don't want to be dropped off in the middle of the desert."

What I wanted was to have our comfortable life back. I cuddled into Mama and kissed her cheek.

"Dora, you cuddle your mother all the time. I think you are getting too old for it."

"But Papa, you like your goodnight kiss every night."

He smiled and I could feel once again the old family unity. Whatever happened we had each other.

But things got worse. Hardy came back and joined us and we were crammed into two and a half rooms. Mama hated it, especially the shared kitchen, which she desperately tried to keep clean.

"These people are so dirty. They cook everything in oil. I can't get rid of the smell."

Nevertheless, Papa continued to insist on a spotless white table cloth and starched damask napkins. The contrast between our genteel habits and our impoverished surroundings was truly bizarre. I had the half room which was entirely occupied a bed with an iron bedhead and foot rest. I strapped my toes under it every night before I went to sleep, hoping to improve my instep.

The Stephan Cathedral had finally received a new roof in yellow and black, complete with eagle motive. I would often go in on my way to ballet classes and find a quiet corner to ask God to help me do three pirouettes instead of two, and help my legs to go higher. Then I would hurry back into the busy, hustling streets. I never stopped. Walking was too slow for me – I seemed to run everywhere. I was too busy, busy catching up with life. I had the feeling that I was always short of time and did three things at once – eating, reading, while doing feet exercises under the table. I had to make sure I was not wasting a minute. I had wasted enough time because of the war. I had lost the first vital years of a ballerina's training and was terrified that I would never make them up.

Many times, when my ballet classes finished late, I would look for my father in the *gasthauses* and bars as I passed by. I would usually find him in the *1st Bezirke*, although not in the smart, expensive places anymore. If I thought he had had too much to drink I would coax him to come home with me. I was always surprised when he paid the bill that it was really wasn't all that much. He seemed to get drunk on very little. I tried to be nice but inside I was very angry. I would take him home to the 2nd *Bezirke*, choosing the back streets in the hope of not bumping into anyone we knew. We had to cross the Danube by the narrow wooden bridge; it was only temporary, the main one had been destroyed. As we stumbled over it, I made sure I had one hand firmly on the rail and one arm around my father. I couldn't swim and I was always petrified of falling into the river, but I knew just across the bridge was home. Mama would open the door and we would be safe. She never reproached Papa. She never was angry. She made do with whatever she got. If there were only potatoes she would make them into something tasty. "Nobody can look into your stomach," was one of Papa's favourite sayings. We owed money at all the local shops: the dairy, the butcher, the grocer. We had to avoid them and buy our supplies elsewhere.

But ballet helped me to forget our troubles. I had gradually moved up through the rows and had displaced Susy, and was now sharing the front with Annemarie; sometimes I was alone in the middle. I trained and practised wherever and whenever I could. Even when it was not my turn I would stand behind, following the others.

"Dora, it's not your turn. Get back, you are in our way."

Nothing disturbed me or put me off. I did whatever

was good for me. When the boys had their turn, I joined in with them too. My jumps were higher than theirs. Sometimes I even had the feeling I was flying, going up and up, like when the wind had taken me away all those years ago outside the cathedral in Sofia.

When I became fourteen, I persuaded my parents to let me leave school and study ballet full time. That meant morning and evening training, studying the history of ballet, musical theory and anatomy. I enjoyed anatomy, except the smell of the marinated bodies. I got around it by holding my perfume bottle under my handkerchief and pressing it tightly to my nose. I never used that perfume afterwards – it always reminded me of dead bodies.

The school was expensive but Dia Luca had a professional company of adult dancers, the Luca Ballet, which was hired out for special occasions. Whenever a girl became ill or was unavailable, Dia Luca, knowing my difficulties, would call me in. I was quick; I had a photographic memory and could learn the steps within an hour, which pleased the other dancers because the rehearsals were kept short. I danced in the Casanova Bar, Maxims, and at the opening of various balls and functions. Dia Luca ran her company like a battalion and enforced a stricter discipline than any sergeant-major. Every week, she made the same speech:

"No hanky panky. Nobody's 'friend' will come in close vicinity of rehearsals. Your religion is ballet and I want you to behave like nuns. The only thing I will accept is a grand mistress – showered with jewels and furs, with a chauffeur-driven car waiting at the stage door. But of course, none of you have the qualities required of a grand mistress."

She was hurtfully honest. The girls, including me, were petrified of her.

Dancers were required for the ball scenes in a big costume film called *Sissi*, starring Romy Schneider, and I went with the older girls to the studios in Sievering for an interview. I was very excited. It would mean much needed extra money and I had always wanted to be in a movie. We stood in a row before a desk, where an assistant director wrote down our names and told us how many days we would be needed for.

"How much?" he asked me."

"What do you mean, how much?"

"What do you want for three days?"

"Oh, I don't mind. I just want to be in the film. I'll take whatever you want to give me."

He looked at me contemptuously. "Next please."

I couldn't understand why I didn't get a part. I was ten times better than Monica who had got three days filming. When I asked her why, she put her arm around my shoulder and said kindly, "Never undersell yourself, Dora. If you don't ask for the going rate, they think you are no good."

A few weeks later, when the studio needed dancers for *The Young Empress*, I asked for twice as much as the girl in front of me and I got a bigger part than anyone else. "Dorale, I wish I had a profession, and then I could work and earn money," my mother had said so many times. Now I had a profession.

De Luca had found a theatre that would take her company on a permanent basis and it took up most of her time. Her husband, Bertil, the leading male dancer in her company, more or less ran the school. My earnings were very irregular and most of it was spent on ballet shoes. I dreaded passing the first office cubicle where I was expected to pay before entering the ballet room. Whenever Dia Luca was there she ignored me and let me pass. Bertil always looked as if he was about to say, "When are you going to pay for your classes?" But he never did.

The secretary was the problem, "Dora, you haven't paid for weeks now. When are you intending to?"

I always had the same excuse ready, "My father wasn't at home. I'll pay tomorrow." I made every effort to be the first to arrive and made sure I was the last to leave so none of the other pupils would hear. But in the ballet room I forgot all my problems. I felt like a queen. Nothing could touch me and I grew stronger and stronger. Whenever Dia Luca made a brief visit to the class, she would always give me a little smile and ask me to do some routine for her. Soon Annemarie and I were promoted to the senior class. We were on our way to being professional dancers. Some of the other girls, the richer ones, began to ask me to coach them privately. I willingly agreed; the small amount I charged them was always most welcome. Only the final exams stood between me and my goal. I became more and more withdrawn into myself in my determination to succeed. I wasn't interested in boys. I dressed in tidy check skirts, blouses and knee socks. My hair was in a ponytail with a fringe. I didn't wear make-up except mascara, on my mother's advice. "Now you have your eyes on, Dora!" she would say each morning. But as soon as I started to exercise, the black mascara would run into my sweat and ended up in my towel.

I began to rebel against my father's strict rules: I had to be home at exactly the right time, even though Hardy sometimes stayed out all night; no trousers at meal times – my newly acquired three-quarter length corduroys had to be taken off; tea spoons to be replaced in the saucer, not left in the cup. One day my mind was elsewhere, and after he had repeated his instructions several times, he took my spoon and shattered my saucer with it. I was shocked. He had never done such a thing to me before

"Apologise to your father," Mama said.

I shook my head. I couldn't stand her weakness towards him. For me there was only black and white and no shades of grey.

"If we lose our manners we lose everything," Papa said softly.

Then I understood – what Mama had always understood. It wasn't her weakness it was her strength. I apologised and never left my spoon in my cup again.

Papa was still playing the black market, although on a much smaller scale. He made weekly trips to Munich on what was known as 'the silk-stocking Express'. Munich was surrounded by American Army bases and overflowing with surplus goods, which were freely on

sale, at a price, along Mohlstrasse in the centre of the
city. The only trouble was that you were only allowed
so much per person before you had to pay heavy custom
duties at the border. But Papa had his own special contacts
and his own special system. He would pack his suitcase
with best Viennese coffee and give it to the conductor
of the *Wagons-Lits*, who would give it back to him when
they got to Munich. Papa would sell the coffee and then
repeat the procedure with nylon stockings and American
cigarettes on his return trip, giving the conductor a fair
share of the profit.

One evening, when I went to meet him at the
Westbahnhof, two policemen were grabbing him by the
arms. I was still terrified of uniforms. All I could think of
was to thank God that he didn't have the suitcase in his
hand.

I ran towards him, "Papa, Papa, how was Munich?
How is grandmother?"

One of my grandmothers was dead and the other
was in Israel, but who cared?

His blue eyes twinkled; I think he was proud of me.
"Grandmother is fine. How are your ballet lessons?"

How could anyone suspect anyone having such a
nice family conversation? But the policemen continued
to pull him away.

"What do you want with my Father?"

"Go home; we have some questions to ask him at the
police station."

I refused to leave him; I would never leave him with
men in uniform. I stubbornly waited for him at the

police station while they questioned him. It was after midnight when we walked home together.

"What happened, Papa?"

He laughed. "They changed the conductor."

After that we chatted away happily as if nothing had happened. We never dwelt on bad experiences, we just pushed them aside. But these were Papa's final days in the black market. It ended in 1955 when the Allies finally withdrew and Austria became an independent state. He had to find some other way to make a living.

My ballet training was coming to an end. I needed 600 Schillings to pay for the State Examination, which I didn't have. I finally managed to borrow it from Bruno, an acquaintance of my father's, who owned an espresso bar, which were the latest craze in Vienna. I had no trouble passing the theory and history of ballet. I then had to dance three pieces – classic, folklore and impressionist, with my own choreography – on the stage of the Raimund Theater, before a board consisting of ballerinas, stage designers, directors and teachers. I wasn't afraid of them or the big stage. I used every bit of it. I was completely lost in the dances. It was my world. My classic piece was quick and powerful and my legs were very strong. I jumped on my point for the longest time; my pizzicato was precise and my jumps were unusually high for a girl. I had learnt how to play the castanets and did a Spanish dance for the folklore, and finally performed Salome for the impressionist, trying to be as sexy as I could imagine, without shedding a single veil.

I stirred up quite a bit of commotion, although naturally at the time I knew nothing about it. One of the examiners was Rudolph Marik, the director of the Raimund Theater. He offered me an engagement, with the promise of my own solo, in a small company that would dance in the operettas. Dia Luca was going to be in charge of it. A little solo dance was all very well but I wanted to know more. I asked to see Dia Luca and was granted an audience. She sat on a chair on a podium and I had to sit at her feet.

"Madame Luca, will I become a prima ballerina?"

"Dora, I can't answer that."

"Why not?"

"Your body can change. You can get fat; your bosom could become too big and you could grow too tall."

"If I don't get too fat, and my bosom doesn't become too big, and I don't grow too tall, and if I work and work and work, will I become a prima ballerina?

She looked at me for a long time before she spoke. "Yes, you will."

That was all I wanted to hear. If I continued with my passion for *patisseries* I would be ruined.

12

First Love

I had fulfilled part of my ambition – I had become a professional dancer. The main function of the Raimund was operetta and the dancers intermingled with the singers. Little did I know then, that Johan Heesters, the handsome leading man of the company, who often smiled at me as we passed in the corridor, had been described as 'Hitler's favourite actor,' and was reputed to have given special performances for the SS Guards in Dachau. His daughter, Nicole, an aspiring actress, often came to see him backstage. She was roughly the same age as me and we became friendly. I had followed Mama's advice and never said I was Jewish, I wonder now if she would have been friendly if she had known?

We went into rehearsals. I was attentive and mastered my part in the shortest time. At the first run-through, Dia Luca sat in the auditorium next to the highly successful stage designer, Ferry Windberger. After she had given the company their notes she turned to me.

"Herr Windberger was an adjudicator at your audition. He says you have the most beautiful legs he has ever seen."

He nodded in agreement. I blushed while the other dancers giggled. His ex-wife, Dolores, a well-known

Viennese actress, had had a song specially written about her legs: *'Das mache nur die Beine von Dolores' ('They make only the legs of Dolores')*. I didn't say anything, but when the older girls teased me about it later in the dressing-room, I lost my temper and threw various items on my make-up table in their direction.

Weeks flew by. I was as busy as any sixteen-year old girl could be: rehearsals, practice, practice, rehearsals. I was given a gorgeous costume for the first operetta we danced in – a sort of Arabian fantasy – but my headdress came with a veil attached that covered most of my face. I thought I knew why – pretty I wasn't. My face may not have been beautiful, but my legs were. Herr Windberger himself had said so. What was the use of being good if they can't see who you are? Every day I cut a little piece off the bottom of the veil, it became smaller and smaller until it rested above my eyebrows.

I still went to the Jewish club when I had time and waved many goodbyes when they left by bus to begin their new lives in Israel. I rarely went home during the day and in the evenings I arrived at the theatre early. I often found myself climbing high onto the iron grid in the flies to watch Ferry Windberger instruct his assistants, or touch up any faults in the scenery with a brush at the end of a long stick. He was tall, with dark hair growing white at the temples. His eyes were twinkling and friendly and his deep laugh would float up to me way above him. He was known as the Don Juan of Vienna, and was reported to have had romances with all the attractive girls in the company. I began to be aware of him watching me in the wings as I danced.

There was talk that Ferry Windberger was giving a party after the following evening's performance. I was much younger than everyone else and it never occurred to me that I would be invited; besides I always took the tram and went home directly after the curtain came down.

The next morning, Monica, who had also joined the company, asked me what I was intending to wear.

"I can't go. My mother would be very upset if I came home late."

"Dora, how can you be so stupid? Do you think he invited the entire ballet because he wants to feed us? He's only interested in you."

I was flabbergasted – how can a man with all those possibilities be interested in me? I wasn't pretty; I was shy and withdrawn, except of course on stage, when I was like an animal let out of its cage.

"Monica, my parents will never allow it."

"Leave it to me. I will arrange it."

She went down to the stage door and phoned my mother, and much to my surprise it was arranged.

I went to the party that night in my check skirt and knee length woollen stockings, but I did add a touch more mascara to my eye lashes. I disliked lipstick – it felt like smudged butter to me. I let my hair hang loose and put on my most valuable jewellery: a pair of simple earrings, a present from Hardy. It was hardly the look of a co-ordinated designer. I arrived at Ferry's villa with some of the other girls, who were wearing their very best. I thought the house was beautiful. Ferry had decorated it with fittings and furniture from his film and stage designs. It was a set in itself: paintings everywhere, statues placed discreetly in corners, lit by spotlights, stairs with decorative iron bannisters leading up to the first floor where the party took place. At the end of a very large room was a long table crammed with uncut salami, cheese and other delicious delicacies. On the wall above were swords and daggers arranged in ornate patterns. The party was noisy and everybody drank too much. Dancers are always ravenously hungry after a performance and some couldn't restrain themselves, and took the daggers from their artistically placed positions on the wall and used them to cut and hack the food in a wild and frenzied manner. I felt very uncomfortable being with them and retired to sit on the stairs. What am I doing here? When is somebody going to take me home?

Then I saw Ferry, leaving his rowdy party and stretching his hand towards me. I didn't take it but just looked at him. He sat next to me.

"Dora, when I saw you at the exams, I knew you were special. I gave you higher marks than I have ever given a dancer before; you have a brilliant future in front of you."

We began to talk, or rather he talked – about stage design, costumes and lighting. He knew so much. I began learning from him in the shortest of time. Meanwhile the party was drawing slowly to a close, and when I saw Monica leaving, I jumped up from the stairs to follow her. Ferry got up as well.

"Monica, I will take Dora home."

"That's fine," she beamed, knowingly nodding her head.

He took me by the hand and led me back into the room where the party had taken place. It was in a chaotic shambles. He opened a side door, leading into his bedroom. I felt my body stiffen. I jumped back. There was no way I would go inside there. We stood in the dimly lit, messy room. He drew me towards a settee. My God, what was I going to do? Mama had always told me that a nice Jewish girl must stay a virgin to get the right man in her life, but I didn't want to get married and have babies like all the other Jewish girls. Dia Luca said we must be careful, but losing our virginity when we were old enough would make us mature and we would be able to express more in our dancing. What did she mean old enough? I'd always thought I was too old. I'd been running for years trying to catch up. He bent over me. I became stiffer and more petrified. He kissed me gently on the forehead and held me for what seemed a long time. Then he got up, took my hand, led me down the stairs and drove me home in a silver MG sports car trimmed with red leather. I made him drop me off at the corner, away from the house, in case I bumped into my father returning from one of his nightly excursions.

The next evening there was a huge bunch of red roses on my makeup table. The other girls didn't say anything; by now they were well aware of my ferocious temper. Ferry was waiting for me by the stage door at the end of the performance. He wanted to take me to supper but I insisted on going home. He drove me as before and stopped again at the corner. I held the roses tightly to my breast. He bent over and kissed me on my mouth. It was my first real kiss. It was different to anything that I had imagined. His lips were soft, his tongue parted my own lips and he engulfed me with a force that I thought would suffocate me. I felt desire for the first time, I wanted to lose myself. I dropped the roses on the car's red carpet and held on to him with all my strength, trying not to drown.

All of a sudden he pushed me aside. I looked at him questioningly.

"Dora, you had better go home."

I picked up the roses and ran inside. My mouth was burning. I locked myself into my room and fell on my bed. I knew I couldn't get babies, but it was just like getting babies. I had always wanted my first kiss to be very special, something I would remember for the rest of my life. I had been waiting for that special moment – that special kiss. I put my hand to my lips and kept it there until I had fallen asleep.

In the morning it was difficult to clean my teeth – I didn't want to wash that kiss away.

Our meetings became frequent. He was twenty-three years older than me, old enough to be my father, but it didn't matter. He picked me up from practice classes, from rehearsals, anywhere and everywhere, but whenever I wanted him to stop at a *patisserie* or *konditorei*; he would firmly shake his head. "Doretchen, no!"

'Doretchen': he had even given me a new name. He was a highly successful architect as well as stage designer, and he taught me all the different styles of architecture as we whizzed around the bomb-scarred city in the open top MG. He took me to museums and taught me the various styles of furniture and introduced me to all forms of art. He wanted to improve my mind as well as my dancing. Improving my dancing? I was constantly thinking what Dia Luca had said – you could not express real emotion in your dance unless you have experienced it yourself. One night I finally came to a decision as he stood waiting for me at the stage door.

"Take me to your home."

Dia Luca's husband, Bertil, was leaving the theatre at the same time and watched as we drove away. Ferry drove me to his home and we dined by candlelight at the long table in the big room at the top of the stairs. We were not at all our usual chattering selves – we hardly said a word. We finished eating and he led me over towards a big settee. I was full of anticipation. It all seemed so natural. I wasn't frightened.

It was over very quickly. Was that what it was all about?

"Did I hurt you, Doretchen? Next time it will be better."

My first kiss had been far more memorable.

I lay in his arms for a while, wondering whether Dia Luca was right and if it would make me a better dancer, before he drove me home and dropped me off at the usual corner.

As I walked into the auditorium the following morning, I became aware of angry voices on the stage. Ferry had arrived early to supervise some adjustments to the set and was being confronted by Bertil.

"What on earth do you think you're doing with Dora?"

I had never seen Bertil so angry.

"It's none of your business," Ferry snapped back.

"She's only sixteen. Dia and I are responsible for her."

"She's old enough to know what she wants."

"She has real promise. Don't ruin her.

"I would never do that. I have her best interests at heart."

"I find that hard to believe. You surely have had enough. Leave her alone."

They went on and on, other dancers and singers began to appear. I sat in the stalls, paralysed. They became more and more angry; all of a sudden they began to hit each other. It wasn't like in the movies. They were clumsy, like little boys. The stage hands pulled them apart. I only had wanted it to be apparent in my dancing, but now the entire theatre, even the cleaners, knew I wasn't a virgin any more. I wanted to disappear behind the last row of seats or even hide under the carpet. They were still hurling insults at each other when Dia appeared and stopped the entire fracas with an imperious wave of her hand, before commencing the rehearsal.

Later that morning, she took me aside. "Dora, I am going to phone your father. I will no longer take responsibility for you."

I was very hurt and ashamed. I really loved her, but there was nothing I could say or do.

From then onwards Papa took me home after the performance nearly every evening, but I continued to see Ferry during the day. It was so stimulating being with him. I told him everything I felt and sought his guidance in everything. He gave me self-confidence. I wasn't shy any more. He taught me to walk in everywhere with my head up and to look people straight in the eye. He made special little drawings and sketches for me and would surprise me with presents: a gold chain, a bracelet, a ring. When Papa was away on a trip we managed to have romantic dinners in small, candle-lit restaurants. One night I opened my napkin and a little jewel box fell on to the tablecloth. Inside was a huge, glittering, golden thaler.

The society event of the year, the Grand Opera Ball, took place in February and was formally opened with a Viennese waltz, danced by members of our company. Afterwards we were allowed to change into ball gowns and join the festivities. It was a truly splendid if ostentatious occasion. One was almost blinded by the glitter of gold and diamonds. The ball gowns were overloaded with embroidery and sequins, and layer upon layer of organza, tulle or chiffon. The men were more sober in their white ties and black tails. The chandeliers reflected every movement as they danced. It seemed as if the war, the Gestapo, the hunger, the camps had never existed.

I had designed my own dress and had persuaded the

wardrobe department to make it for me, with shoes and handbag to match. It was in heavy, metal-grey duchesse silk satin, with no décolleté. No sleeves and a dropped waist with little pleats. I had hardly any bosom and small hips and it fitted my figure perfectly. No embroidery or jewels. My hair was swept back with a pearl binding that held my pony tail.

"Doretchen, you are beautiful." Ferry took me by the hand, like Prince Charming, and led me to the dance floor. Later in his bedroom, our love making was even more memorable than that first kiss.

Bertil and Dia Luca had relaxed a little about our relationship, and Ferry began to drive me home again. Sometimes we would stop for a snack at Maxim, a nightclub which he was re-designing, but everything we did had to fit in with my plans. I would never miss a class, or a rehearsal or a teaching commitment. There was never enough time for us to be together. The Easter/Pesach holiday finally provided us with an opportunity. There was a break at the theatre and the Gordonia Club were going on a camp. I told my parents I was going with them, but instead went away for a few days with Ferry. We drove in his little MG to Salzburg, Innsbruck and into Switzerland. It was the first time I had ever seen towns untouched by the war. We spent the Easter weekend at a charming little hotel on the banks of Lake Geneva.

He woke me on Easter Morning. "Doretchen, the Easter Bunny has been here and left you some things in the garden. You'd better go and find them."

I had barely heard of the Easter Bunny, but I forgot all about being a grown-up. Our room was on the ground floor with French windows. I opened them and ran into the hotel garden like a child, looking under bushes and trees and chairs, trying to find my presents. I found small eggs and little bunnies, but Ferry kept encouraging me to look further until, hidden among the reeds around the lake, I discovered a yellow carton. Inside was a big chocolate egg. Inside of that was a beautiful ring set with a huge pink coral. I ran to him and threw my arms around his neck; he picked me up and carried me back into our room.

When we returned home I felt that I finally was no longer a child. I was a woman to Ferry, and we loved each other. Even so, I didn't show Mama the ring, although I told her about Ferry and where I had really been. She wasn't angry – how could she have so much patience with me?

"Dorale, if you do it, it cannot be bad."

"Mama, were you ever in love before you married Papa?"

She gave a shy smile. "Of course."

"Who was it? How did it happen?"

"He was a Hussar. He passed by our window every morning on his horse. I used to push the curtains aside and we would wave to one another."

"Yes? …And what next?"

"And then I met your father."

It only proved how bad I was. I would never be able to marry a Jewish man and make my parents happy. I wanted to continue with my busy, hectic life. Mama always used to say, "You have *spilkes* in the *tuches*" ('ants in the pants'). She was right.

Hardy now considered himself to be completely grown-up and was hardly ever at home. He began to come to the theatre to watch me and of course the other girls. He got himself a Vespa and he took me for rides on it through the Vienna Woods. I clung on to him imagining I was Audrey Hepburn in *Roman Holiday*. It eventually got him into trouble when he forgot to get a licence and he ended up at the police station. He couldn't get out unless he paid a heavy fine, which he didn't have. Papa was away and I only had about half of the amount required. There was nothing for it but to visit Bruno in his expresso bar again. Luckily, I had paid back my previous loan very quickly, and he gave me the money without compunction. I then went to the police station and got my big brother out of gaol. I was no longer his little sister.

Papa still struggled to make a living. He obtained a large quantity of bed sheets and hawked them from door to door. He didn't sell a single one. They remained piled in the apartment for months.

Though I was now a fully professional dancer at the Raimund, we were only really doing little dances to enliven the proceedings. It was still my ambition to be a leading dancer in a renowned company, performing the great classical ballets such as *Swan Lake* and *Giselle* and *The Nutcracker*. My chance came when the Vienna

State Opera decided to reform its ballet company and perform in the Volksoper until the grand Opera House was rebuilt. Dia Luca was to be the choreographer and duly appointed me as coryphée, the position below a solo dancer. I was the youngest girl in the company and Annemarie was only in the *corps de ballet*. I had overtaken her at last.

I found it very different to the relaxed atmosphere at the Raimund. The other girls were the best they could find, chosen from all over Austria, all very ambitious, fighting for a place on the narrow ladder to the top. Our daily routine began at 8 am with training, then lunch between 12 and 2, solo rehearsals or studying new ballets took up the afternoons and often went on late into the evenings until the point of exhaustion. Dancers then, especially the men, were not the athletes that they are today. We had no sprung floors to practice on; no air-controlled rehearsal rooms; we knew little about diet and health food, but we managed somehow and I was always ready for more. Whenever I was free, I would dash to have private classes from a Russian ballerina, who had danced with Pavlova. She was very old and could only move with a stick, which she would use to tap our legs if they were not in the right position. There was no piano in her little studio and she sang out the rhythm in her crackling voice. There were usually only two girls in her class, three at the most, and nothing escaped her eagle eyes. It was a painful and tedious hour, but my technique gradually improved and I counted myself lucky to train under her.

Everything was working out as I had dreamed. Whenever a rehearsal time was changed or cancelled, I would pick up the phone, and if Ferry was free he would come and pick me up, although more and more often, he was too busy working at the Raimund. In that case I would go back home to Mama and happily darn my ballet shoes, or pick the ladders out of my tights with a crochet hook, and talk about the latest news of the family in Israel. My life seemed to be perfect.

One morning, we were training in our usual manner when Dia Luca came in with a short little man. She told us to continue working. The man remained at the door with his hat on as his eyes wandered from girl to girl. After a while he pointed at me and they went out. At the break I was summoned to Dia Luca's office.

"Dora, Maestro Hindemith saw you this morning, and has chosen you to dance the lead in his new work, *Neues vom Tage.*"

I didn't know who Hindemith was, but it sounded too good to be true.

"Does it mean I am now a solo dancer and will get more money?"

She laughed and gave me a little kiss on my cheek.

I was ecstatic, life could not be better. All my dreams had come true. I rushed to phone Ferry. I couldn't wait to tell him the news. The telephone seemed to ring for ages. He picked it up at last.

"Ferry…"

"Doretchen, there's something I have to tell you…"

"Yes, yes, but first you must listen to me…"

"No, please. I have been seeing a lot of Inga lately. I think I am in love with her. It is better you know now."

Inga? I couldn't believe it. He was making a terrible mistake. She was the most untalented dancer at the Raimund. She hadn't been invited to join the Volksoper ballet. She had big eyes like a cow and dyed black hair, and dyed so badly that everyone could see it was dyed. On top of that she had a bad reputation with men. How dare he prefer her to me! Now I understood his busy evenings at the Raimund. How immature and gullible I had been. Everyone must have known except me. If he had told me the news to my face I would have killed him.

"How can you hurt me like this?" I screamed. "Don't you know I love you?"

"Doretchen, you must understand. I am with her now."

I slammed the telephone down. I would show him. I would be the biggest success ever. I didn't realise how immature I still was.

I ran crying to the only person who could comfort me. "Mama, Mama, how could she take him from me? Everybody knew we were together."

"Baby, Mousela, you will get over it. Time cures everything."

"But it hurts. It hurts me."

"There is nothing you can do. You must wait until the pain goes away. It takes time."

"But how much time? I want to prepare myself for how long I have to suffer."

It would take a long time; a very long time. I had loved Ferry with all the innocence and fervour of a sixteen-year-old girl. I only had wanted to be with him. But at least, I still had my other love, the ballet.

My salary had gone up to 1,800 Schillings but it was still less than the solo dancers. It was barely possible, but I worked harder than ever before. The new part with Hindemith's tonal music was very difficult. The rhythm was forever changing, I was constantly counting – it was more like mathematics. There was little melody to hold on to. The most difficult moment was at the end of the ballet; 22 *rond de jambe,* with *double* in between, which meant doing 44 in the rehearsal room. When the rehearsal room was busy I would practice alone on the cement floor of the foyer. I had sticking plaster around practically every toe and they were often covered in blood, but I continued, harder and harder, as if wanting to hurt myself into forgetting my first love. I began to eat too much to the concern of Gerhardt, my partner, the leading male soloist, and was reprimanded by Dia Luca. I took pills to reduce my appetite, and went through the day with just a pot of yoghurt and a cigarette, but all too often, after the performance at night, I would go mad and stuff myself with food. Then I would feel guilty and take three or four laxative pills, to empty myself for the next morning. I never did anything in moderation, but one thing I promised myself was that I would never love anyone so completely again. I would never be utterly reliant on a man. I would be my own person.

13

New Steps

I was the youngest solo dancer ever and was promoted to a dressing room on the first floor, with my own dresser, who I all too soon discovered disliked me utterly. A good dresser is vital in the ballet: a shoe can easily break and quick changes have to be exact and swift, the music won't wait. I was very particular and gave her all my instructions in great detail. I always insisted on checking my costumes, but at the first dress rehearsal they were not laid out as I had asked, and she mixed them up during the quick changes. I was sure she had done it on purpose. She seemed to spend most of the evening gossiping with the other dressers in the corridor.

"Dora is a typical Jew," I overheard her mutter one on occasion; "she is all elbows."

It was a typical Viennese expression. It was people like her who had watched and jeered as the Jews were forced to scrub the pavements on their knees. I ignored it – I was on stage, not her.

My big opening night came: Friday 13th. I was in my dressing room early as usual, reading my good luck cards. Dia Luca had written: "Your technique is good, but you must work on your character." I was pondering what she meant when the porter came in with a huge bunch of red roses. There was no card.

"There's a telephone call waiting for you downstairs from Mr Windberger."

My heart jumped: after all those weeks of pain. But I couldn't talk to him now; it would upset me too much. I had to think only of my performance.

"Please, tell him I'm too busy."

The curtains opened, the chorus began to sing. I waited in the wings with Gerhardt. We were both dressed in grey leotards from top to bottom. I had a piece of material in various shades of grey around my hips, with a sort of tail floating behind me. Our cue came and we stepped into a box which was pushed into the middle of the stage. Another cue and we sprang out of our enclosure with spotlights catching our bodies and following every movement. It all went perfectly. I felt great. I could sense that the audience was completely in my hands; they applauded every one of my 22 *rond de jambe* and broke into a crescendo at the end. The curtains fell and opened again and again. Gerhardt and I were called in front to receive yet more applause and bouquets of flowers. I felt exuberant, all my pain and unhappiness had been worthwhile. I went up the stairs back to my dressing room, took off my costume and showered. There was a knock on the door. I wasn't sure if I wanted it to be Ferry or not.

"Come in."

A little man entered. For a moment I didn't know who he was, then Maestro Hindemith took off his hat – he was bald.

"You were magnificent," was all he said.

As I came down to the stage door, a woman with peroxided blonde hair was waiting for me. "Fraulein Reisser, I am a ballet teacher. I just wanted to tell you how wonderfully you danced tonight." It was the woman who had turned me down for the Opera school; the one who had so nearly ruined my dream.

Next morning I went to Dia Luca's office and asked for my salary to be equal to that of the other solo dancers.

She smiled. "Of course. You are now my little prima ballerina."

I had become one of the attractions – a large photo of me was hung up in the lobby. Papa had always pretended to be disinterested in my dancing, but Hardy told me that some nights, before the performance, Papa would stand in the lobby staring up at my photo. He hoped that somebody would ask him who he was looking at, so he could reply, "My daughter."

It was a beautiful summer's day, Ferry had never rung again and despite my success I was still struggling to get over him. I had finished practice and was on the wooden bridge, crossing over the Danube on my way to see Mama, my little black leather suitcase with my ballet shoes in my hand. Strange, I thought, the river didn't scare me anymore. The famous 'Blue Danube' was a joke. It was muddy and brown. But then, the Viennese didn't go in for realism; they preferred to live with their stale memories. As far as I could see, they had no curiosity of mind or hunger for fresh knowledge. Freud had had both in abundance, but he was Jewish and had escaped. The Viennese were stuck in the past and were definitely in need of new ideas.

I took out my keys and opened the door to the flat. It still smelt of the Greeks' cooking. I went along the dark corridor and opened the door into what we called our sitting room. The smell of cooking vanished in an instant: a vase of beautifully scented pink roses was on the table. My parents and Hardy were drinking tea with a strange man. He was quite young, despite his receding hairline.

Mama was looking very happy. "Dorale, this is your cousin, Benno."

I couldn't recognise him from the photos Mama had kept from Istanbul. I had always thought of him as a beautiful blonde baby with lots of curls. I hoped baldness didn't run in the family – I had enough problems with my hair already.

"Hello, Benno." I kissed him on the cheek.

He looked very American, which was hardly surprising as Aunt Sophie had immigrated to America when he had been very young and he had been brought up in Brooklyn. None of us could speak English to him so we struggled with Yiddish and French. We gathered he had been a social worker, but was now a financial genius who had come to Europe with a brilliant new idea that would make everyone rich. He spoke very softly but with great fervour, it was if he were preaching a new religion. Papa, who was working in a friend's restaurant at the time, looked decidedly sceptical, but Hardy was completely fascinated.

The next day I took my new-found cousin for a walk around the town.

"What is this business that is going to make everyone rich?"

"Selling mutual funds to American Servicemen in Europe, who would not normally invest in stocks and shares. Why should only the rich get richer from the market? Small investors should also have the chance."

"What are mutual funds?" I was ashamed of my ignorance.

"If you have enough money you invest in all the best companies. A few will go down, but the market always rises eventually. A mutual fund does that for you. You can't lose"

He bought me a pink rose at a flower stand and a copy of his favourite book, *Le Petit Prince,* before taking me for coffee and cakes at Demel's. I was in paradise and forgot all about my stupid diet, although I was quite shocked when Benno began to take off his jacket. Gentlemen didn't do that in Vienna, but he had no time for old rules and customs. He asked me if I would like to join him in Geneva for a few days if he sent me a ticket.

I kissed his cheek. "When I get some time off, I would love to come."

He saw me dance that night. After the performance a great bunch of the same fragrant roses was delivered to my dressing room. This time there was a card: *'To a beautiful girl, with thanks for a beautiful performance, Bernie.'*

Papa's new plan was to open a *gasthaus* with yet another friend. It was far from the city centre and he and Mama would have to move there and share accommodation in the friend's flat. It would have been impossible for me to live so far out, and so I rented a little room two minutes from the Opera – a corner room with two windows, bright and tidy, in an apartment owned by an elderly couple who took a parental interest in me.

My parent's new home was even worse than that before. There was no privacy, everything was shared and everything was dirty. My heart bled for my poor mother when I went to visit her. She escaped to spend every Sunday with me. We would walk in the nearby park and then buy salami and bread, and I would serve it in my room on a tray with tea, like we used to at home. She was looking older, her health was not good, and the war and the years in Vienna had taken their toll. She had had to cope with so much pain and suffering. Nevertheless, she was overflowing with love and we had precious, peaceful moments together. She would hold my hand so lovingly and her soft voice was full of wisdom.

"Dorchika, when you chose a husband remember that the money may go, but the man stays. People talk too much of the past and how rich and how successful they once were. How they lived and what they did. Who cares? It's now that counts. Cope with the present; what is gone is gone. Don't cry for it, everything passes, but never forget who you are and where you came from. You will always have yourself to be proud of, or to blame. Even if you lose everything in life, never lose your dignity. It is irreplaceable. You must be able to look at yourself in the mirror and be proud of what you see."

All she wanted was for me to have a happy and a settled life, but marriage remained the furthest thing from my mind. Most of the other girls at the ballet lived with their parents or boyfriends and were well taken care of, but I was determined to manage on my own. My earnings were just enough for my accommodation, food, classes, and my clothes, which I was becoming more and more conscious of. I had a wardrobe many young ladies would have considered themselves fortunate to own. It didn't matter that they were only copies from famous designers, on me they looked real. Luckily I had been born with a sense of style, or perhaps it came from Mama, but I knew instinctively what looked good on me. I found that I could make expensive looking outfits from the cheapest things. I had a fetish for shoes and sometimes spent more on them than the rest of my attire.

My weight was still a problem, but I managed somehow to control it. My nose was a different matter, to my and my mother's surprise, it grew and grew. It changed from being my mother's nose into my father's, and I became increasingly conscious of it. Nose operations in Vienna were then in their very early stages. I knew of only one girl who had had one. I got the address of the doctor from her, and arranged an appointment. He seemed to be a kind and sympathetic man. I told him I had no money for the operation, but I needed it desperately for my profession. He quite taken aback, but was impressed by my determination and cheek, and said that if I agreed to let him put a photo of my profile, before and after the operation, in a medical magazine, he would do it for nothing. I had to have a signed agreement from my parents as I was not yet eighteen. I asked my mother, as I knew she would be the easier to persuade. She wanted to accompany me to the hospital, but I preferred to do it on my own. Only one problem remained – the Opera would not give me time off unless I was sick. I told them I was suffering from acute appendicitis, and persuaded the very obliging doctor to take out my appendix at the same time as he reshaped my nose.

When I awoke after both operations, I was in pain from top to bottom, but couldn't wait to see myself in a mirror. It was a horrible sight: my eyes were blue and swollen and my nose was covered with a huge white plaster. I had to wait impatiently for several days until the plaster was removed and my new profile emerged.

"You are beautiful," the doctor said. "With your smile and beauty you will be a star."

But I knew that beauty wasn't enough to make you a star in the ballet. You had to work.

One Sunday Mama didn't come to visit me. Nobody had phoned during the week and there was no phone in the flat where they were living. When I went to see her on the following Sunday I found her alone, lying ill in bed, in the cramped dirty room that also served as a kitchen. She looked terrible.

"Where is Papa?"

"I don't know."

I went to a phone box in the street and phoned our old family doctor, Dr Spomberger, the father of my old school friend, Christel. I told him it was urgent and he arrived on his crutches shortly after. He prescribed medicine, but was shocked at the squalor.

"Frau Reisser, you must move out of here. This is not a place for you."

How right he was. My God, why did this gentle woman never complain? I was furious. I found my father in the bar of the *gasthaus*, and finally confronted him. It seemed he couldn't face anything anymore.

"Dorale, you must understand, I am going through a bad time."

"For God's sake, Papa, stop running away. Do something. She is your wife!"

I looked at him, loving him, not wanting to lose my respect for him. It would take years before I fully understood what he had been going through. He had come to Bulgaria with nothing and ended up being one of the richest men in Sofia. He had been robbed of everything and after his brutal incarceration he had tried to recapture his old spirit and resilience. It had worked for a while but, although he was still hungry for life, the strength had been drained out of him. My heart opened to him once more and I kissed his hand, which I made wet with my tears. Eventually he agreed that he would find accommodation near the Opera where Mama and I could live together.

We rented two rooms in an old lady's apartment, in fact one and a half rooms. I had the small one and the larger one, where we also ate and lived, was Mama's. My earnings were barely adequate – I gave Mama money for food and our daily expenses, the remainder went on ballet shoes, which I went through at an alarming rate.

Her health soon improved, thanks to Dr Spomberger's medicine and being out of the grime and filth, and I was so happy to be with her again. Life was so much easier. She took care of me in her usual way and I didn't have to bother with household chores. There was always a meal waiting for me whenever I came home, and I could talk and tell her everything. She would always listen, whatever the time, day or night. She loved showing me the letters from her sisters in Israel and America. She had sent them cuttings from the papers of my performances and they were now congratulating her on my achievements, instead of sending commiserations for having a dancer as a daughter. Papa would drop in sometimes and open a bottle of sparkling *Sekt*, and we would drink and reminisce. They were pleasant times; we were briefly united again, hoping for a better life together.

14

Fruit and Vegetables and Coffee

That autumn, Hardy took me to the WIZO (Women's International Zionist Organization) ball. There had been 180,000 Jews in Vienna before Hitler marched in. Two thirds had managed to escape but 65,000 had died. The post-war Jewish population was therefore a very close-knit society and all of the leading lights were going to be there. I had designed my own gown, in black and white duchesse silk satin, which I had once again persuaded the wardrobe to make for me. I was sitting confidently on a high chair at the bar, even though I knew that Papa would have disapproved, when one of my students came towards me.

"Fraulein Reisser, may I introduce you to my father, Carlos Fluss?"

The man beside her was quite short but extremely good-looking, with smooth black hair, deep deer-like eyes and soft delicate lips. His suit was extremely well cut and hung perfectly on his body, unlike Ferry, who was very relaxed about his clothes and usually wore pullovers.

He sat on the bar stool next to me and ordered champagne and we talked into the small hours: what I liked, what I didn't like, what I wanted to be. He seemed to know a lot about everything, but opera and music were his special loves. When my brother came to take me home, Carlos insisted that it would be his pleasure, much to Hardy's relief as he was in pursuit of his latest girl. Carlos led me outside to a gleaming new Ferrari, opened the door for me most graciously, and drove me home in it. As we said goodnight at the door, he bent his head and kissed my hand in the old gentlemanly manner. He waited until the light was turned on in my room before the Ferrari roared away. I was happy and exhilarated. It had been a lovely ball and I had had a gentleman as my companion. I took off my clothes, folded them neatly on the chair and snuggled into my eiderdown, holding my little pillow close to my breast.

Next morning, Carlos's daughter rang me at the theatre.

"Fraulein Reisser, my father has two tickets tonight for Vivien Leigh at the Burgtheater; would you like to go with me?"

I couldn't believe it. Vivien Leigh, one of my favourite actresses ever since I had seen *Gone with the Wind*, was in Vienna with her husband, Sir Laurence Olivier, the greatest actor in the world, and it was impossible to get tickets.

"But surely your father wants to go?"

"No. Shakespeare is too heavy for him. He prefers plays with music."

I wasn't dancing that evening and accepted at once. It was a grand occasion. Anyone who was anyone was there. It was as if Vienna had been accepted back among the world's civilised cities again. I must admit that I was slightly disappointed with the play, *Titus Andronicus*, which was very brutal and which I found impossible to follow. Moreover, my idol, Vivien Leigh, had very little to do. She hardly spoke, which wasn't surprising as she had her tongue cut off very early in the proceedings. Laurence Olivier was not the handsome, vibrant, romantic actor I remembered from *Wuthering Heights* and *Rebecca*, but a grumpy old man, who as far as I could see cut off his own hand for no reason, and then killed his enemy's sons and then served them up to her cooked in a pie. I found it all quite exhausting. After the play, Carlos's daughter invited me to join her in the Burg coffee house. I declined because I had practice the following morning and didn't want to get home late.

"My father is waiting in the coffee house for us. He will be very disappointed. He arranged everything so that he could see you again."

I could hardly believe it. We went into the coffee house, Carlos gave his daughter a goodbye kiss and we were alone. We talked again; or rather he talked as I ate my patisserie, before he drove me home in the Ferrari. He kissed my hand as before and asked if he could pick me up after my performance the following evening.

"If you want to, but it would be easier to walk, I live so close."

"I will be there."

The next night I came out of the stage door and looked for the Ferrari. There was no sign of it, only an enormous American car, such as I had only seen in the movies. Carlos got out.

"Good evening," he kissed my hand. "Have you eaten?"

"No." I was starving as I always was after a performance. "But I'm not dressed to go anywhere."

"We will go to a little place I know in Grinzing. You can wear whatever you like there."

I ate too much *wurst*; he drank wine, and then drove me home as before.

The following evening he arrived in a Mercedes. I hadn't given it much thought, but I was convinced he must be a car dealer. We went to another delightful restaurant and again I ate too much. He drove me home with the customary kiss on my hand. I didn't see him for two weeks, but I received postcards from Milan, Venice and Turin, with fondest regards but no signature. I began to wonder who he actually was. Had he gone there to pick up more cars? I couldn't phone his daughter, so I popped into Bruno's espresso bar. Bruno always knew everything.

"You mean Carlos Fluss, the fruit and vegetable king?"

"Fruit and vegetable king? What does that mean? What a stupid expression."

"There's nothing stupid about it. He has whole streets of warehouses. Most of the fruit and vegetables eaten in Vienna come out of them. He has monopolised the market."

So Carlos Fluss was in vegetables not cars. Obviously cars were only his very expensive hobby.

That evening, as I came out of the stage door to take a deep breath of the fresh evening air,

"*Guten abend, Dora.*"

I turned and he was standing there. He took me in his arms and kissed me for the first time. There was no longer fresh evening air on my face, only his hot kiss, almost suffocating me. And in front of everyone: the other dancers were constantly coming out past us. They must have been stunned. I thought he had lost his mind and disentangled myself and got into his car. We didn't talk on the short drive to my front door.

"Dora, I haven't stopped thinking about you. I've never felt like this before."

"Carlos, you are married."

"I will leave her."

I knew he couldn't. Bruno had told me his wife was a vital part of his business.

"It will never work. Goodnight." I began to get out of the car.

"Wait. I have brought you something from Italy."

He opened the back of the car and took out a big suitcase and carried it to the front door.

"A suitcase? Why do I need a suitcase?"

He said nothing but kissed my hand as he always did and drove away.

The case was heavy. What could be inside it? I lugged it up to my room and opened it with anticipation. I was immediately dazzled by reams of the brightest coloured silk, satin and the softest of wool – so delicate and beautiful. My dressmaker at the theatre was going to be extremely busy. I took them out and threw them around my little room – they floated in the air like the most gorgeous parachutes. A wine-red silk box fell on to the floor. Inside was a very unusual brooch: green leaves on a stalk of pearls.

The next evening the largest bunch of roses I'd ever seen was waiting for me at the stage door – too many to count. Orchids arrived every evening after that, together with baskets of fruit, so heavy that I could not lift them, and box after box of chocolates. I shared everything with the other dancers, who duly appreciated Carlos's generosity. He was at the stage door nearly every evening, to take me to the most elegant restaurants in Vienna. Carlos was the most persistent man I have ever met, and also the most romantic. How could he not have been with his mixture of Italian and Jewish blood? If the restaurant had a violin and piano, he would arrange for them to play the theme from Ingrid Bergman's film *Intermezzo*, as we walked in. He didn't appear to worry if anyone saw us together and reported it to his wife, even though Vienna was just like a village and gossip a favourite Viennese pastime.

One night Carlos took me to the Red Bar at the Hotel Sacher, where Papa had often taken me for *Tafelspitzer* in his wealthier days. The *maître d'* recognised me immediately:

"How is your father, Fraulein Reisser? I haven't seen him for a long time."

"Thank you. He is very well. He travels a lot." I lied.

Some Sundays Carlos would drive out to the

vineyard on the Cobenzl, with is breath-taking views of Vienna and the Danube, and we would sit before a roaring log fire and sip *Grüner Veltliner,* the local wine. He would never let go of my hand, although we never made love.

I didn't need a lot of sleep. I had boundless energy. I could rehearse, exercise, perform and was always ready to go out every night and not come home until early morning. My character didn't seem to change. I still had outbursts of temper, even on stage. One night, during *Carmen*, I smashed my tambourine through my poor partner's head. Another time, when I was doing pirouettes on his finger, I screamed at him, in the middle of a performance, because he was putting me off balance. I demanded perfection from myself and everyone around me. Some partners, such as Gerhardt, loved dancing with me, others hated it. There was nothing in between.

Dudi Deutsch was introduced to me by Mindo, a girl friend from the Gordonia-Maccabi Hatzair, who had recently married at the age of seventeen. Most Jewish girls married young in Vienna at that time, and Mindo thought Dudi would be a suitable husband for me. He was in his mid-thirties, small and stocky and he wore glasses. Not what you would call a good-looking man, but he definitely knew how to enjoy the best things in life. He came from a very wealthy religious family who imported most of the coffee into Vienna, and Vienna certainly drunk a lot of coffee. If Carlos was King of Fruit and Vegetables, Dudi was surely Prince of Coffee.

He began to take me out, even though I was still seeing Carlos. He took me to the most fashionable places in Vienna: the Eden Bar, Trummelhof, and Splendid. He loved dancing, music ran through his veins. Some mornings, when I was free, he took me riding in the Prater. I had always loved horses. They were the only things I could draw at school. Riding came naturally to me, and unlike skiing or skating I didn't have to worry about harming my legs. Dudi showered me with presents and sent my mother flowers and did all the right things. He decided he was in love with me and duly took me home one Friday evening to meet his mother. I wore a simple black dress with a plain silver chain around my neck and tried desperately to behave properly, but I could feel her dislike and disapproval instantly. I could almost see balloons of her thoughts coming out of her head, like in the comics:

'A dancer in the family! Unheard of!'

'Is she really Jewish?'

'She doesn't even know the prayers!'

Dudi's younger brother was there with his quiet orthodox wife dutifully wearing a scarf. That would never be for me. I couldn't wait to get out and head for the Eden Bar.

We had good times but Dudi gradually became possessive and jealous and sought to dominate my life. He wanted to know exactly what I was doing during the day and had his chauffeur and car waiting for me wherever I went, even for the shortest of distances: across the road to the coffee house for lunch; back to the rehearsal room, or from my home to the Opera. I would have much preferred to walk with my friends but the chauffeur was always there. I began to play games and slip out of the Opera by the front door, and telephone Dudi from a box to tell him exactly where I was and where the chauffeur was parked. I loved my freedom and didn't want to give it up.

It was a Friday, I had no performance and Dudi decided to escape his mother's dinner and take me to the casino at Baden, a pretty spa town, twenty odd kilometres from Vienna. The casino, which until recently had been the headquarters of the Soviet forces, was truly a palace. We drove through beautiful gardens and up a ramp to a covered portico, where Dudi was welcomed by the owner himself. He was obviously a valued customer. Inside, everything was luxurious and civilised; it was like stepping back into the days of the Emperor Franz Joseph. After a splendid dinner we went to the roulette table where I watched Dudi play. He offered me some chips, but I refused. I knew how hard it was to make money and thought it wrong to waste so much on a stupid bouncing little ball. I was wearing pearl earrings that Dudi had given me, but my simple black dress had Carlos's pearl broach upon it. The main door opened and a noisy, flamboyant crowd burst in. I was shocked to see that Carlos was amongst them. I hadn't seen him for several weeks. We stared at each other. Dudi noticed immediately and took me by the arm to another room. It was dimly lit, apart from the light over the Baccarat table. There was only one empty place. Dudi sat down, and a chair was placed for me behind him. Dudi ordered champagne and began to play.

"Punto."

Carlos walked in, saw that the table was full, and whispered something into the croupier's ear. The seat opposite Dudi was vacated in the shortest of time. I stiffened. Carlos glared at Dudi. Dudi glared at Carlos. They were preparing for a duel.

"Banco."

"Punto."

The tension grew and seemed to penetrate everyone around the table. The other players dropped out one by one. Soon it was only Carlos and Dudi, playing against each other, oblivious of all else around them, passing the dealing shoe back and forth between themselves.

"Banco."

"Punto."

Dudi was losing but wouldn't give in. I wished his credit hadn't been so good. I was faint with strain and anxiety, but neither Carlos nor Dudi would look at me. Their eyes were only on each other or the cards on the table. I didn't know who I wanted to win. More and more people were coming in to watch. The owner saw my distress and led me to the bar in the centre of the main room.

"Have a glass of champagne. It will calm you down."

"Can't you stop it?"

"Fraulein Reisser, it's better not to interfere."

"But you don't understand what's happening."

"I understand very well, Fraulein Reisser."

I couldn't talk any more. I sat at the bar and waited. It seemed ages until Dudi came out of the Baccarat room and sat on the stool beside me. He laughed and kissed me.

"More champagne?"

"Dudi, how much did you lose?"

"Lose? I didn't lose." He took my hand and kissed it passionately.

But he had no chips to cash at the till and he signed the bill when we left. He drove back to Vienna and held me close to him as we danced at the Eden Bar before he took me to his apartment. We slept together that night. He was an extraordinary passionate lover. We woke late and his butler brought us our breakfast in bed.

That autumn of 1956, two events occurred that made me realise albeit briefly, how shallow my life had become. The Hungarian revolution, the first post-war uprising against Soviet power, broke out on October 23rd, to be followed a few days later by the Israeli invasion of the Sinai Peninsula, more commonly referred to as 'The Suez Crisis'. Mama and I were desperately worried about Aunt Fanny and all the rest of them in Israel. Would they ever find peace? The border with Hungary was little more than fifty kilometres away. Mindo's husband was Hungarian and went with others to help family and friends in Budapest. Jews always draw close together in times of trouble, and they have had more than their share of trouble. I forgot the bars and nightclubs; for a week or two even the ballet didn't seem important. I sat up with Mindo, listening fearfully to the radio as the Russian tanks poured in to squash the rebels, until her husband escaped back over the border and came safely home.

15

Moving On

Gertie and Lisle were my two special girlfriends in the ballet. Gertie had thick blonde hair, a lovely little Viennese nose, a charming smile and a good figure. She had many admirers and took life as it came. Although she was a coryphée, her dancing wasn't the best, but she smiled a lot, she was generous and uncomplicated and people loved her. Her family were quite well-off, she had three older brothers and Gertie was the only daughter. There was nothing in life that Gertie seemed to be missing. Lisle was in the *corps de ballet*. She was Jewish and her father held a high position, a police doctor, in the local government. She was an only child and was extremely spoilt. She didn't have much to give to the ballet and didn't seem to care much about it anyway. Her main concern was her beauty, which she had in abundance. Her hair, which she bound with a silk scarf behind her neck, was as black and shiny as a raven's wing. Her eyes were smiling and she was full of life and curiosity. She was constantly giggling, life seemed only a joke to her, but I knew that inside she was confused – not knowing where she was going or what she wanted. She told me, years and years later, that she had survived the concentration camp at Theresienstadt, where 33,000

141

inmates had been murdered or had died of malnutrition or disease.

"My father was picked up first. The Gestapo always came at night. Mother and I walked the streets of Vienna all through the night and slept in doorways to avoid them; but one evening the Gestapo came early."

"Lisle, why did you never tell me?"

"Dora, did you ever tell me what happened to you?"

"No. I was told not to talk about it.

"And so was I."

(*Lisle eventually made a filmed testimony of her experiences for Stephen Spielberg's Shoah Foundation.*)

Heidi, a solo dancer like me, was older and had worked years to reach the top of the ladder and was determined to stay there. We had a love/hate relationship. We trained together, took private classes together, and competed against each other non-stop. She looked like a ballet dancer – straight, long black hair over her ears, held fast in a comb at the back. She never had a problem with her weight – she was always slim – but my ankles were far more delicate.

"Dora, did you know that Inga and Ferry Windberger have married, and she is having a baby?" Heidi informed me very brightly one morning.

I went home, took all his presents, the gold thaler, the coral ring, bracelets, his little letters and drawings, everything, and put them in a shoe box. He was now finally dead for me. I never wanted to hear his name uttered before me again. All that remained was the love of art and architecture that he had given me.

A company, putting together a programme of Viennese operetta for a tour of Italy and Sicily during the summer break, was looking for dancers, and Lisle, Gertie and I signed up immediately. The performance schedule was easy; it was a holiday with pay. The first stop was a big open-air theatre in Turin, then Milan and then Rome, then Genoa, then Catania. We promised we would look after each other and do everything together, like the three musketeers. We shared a room and laughed and chatted until late at night, we discovered Campari and thought it was the most chic and sophisticated thing. In the shortest of time everybody on the tour knew all about us and we were invited to every party and occasion. Italian men smiled and whistled at us and we pretended not to care. I had never been to Italy before and loved it. We got to Rome and had ice cream on the Spanish Steps, visited St Peter's, made wishes and sang Frank Sinatra's song as we threw coins into the Trevi Fountain, and did all the things that other tourists do. We were having a completely happy, carefree time until Lisle made an unexpected announcement.

"Gertie, Dora, I'm pregnant."

"Oh my God! And you're not married!"

"Why didn't you tell us in Vienna?" Gertie demanded.

"I didn't know for sure. I'm not regular."

"If you're not regular it may come."

"It should have come by now."

I sat there stunned. I was on my second lover but I really had no idea about such matters. I had left it all to my more experienced partners. What should we do?

Definitely not tell the parents. "Lisle, I really don't know what to do, but we must do something. We have three weeks before we get back to Vienna."

"But what can we do?" said Lisle pitifully.

"Hot bath and vodka." Gertie was the more experienced and practical.

"Yes, Gertie. I saw that in a movie," I exclaimed enthusiastically.

"I saw that movie too," wailed Lisle. "It didn't work."

"That was only a movie. It will work for us." Gertie was always an optimist like me.

After the performance that night, we bought a large bottle of vodka on our way back to our *pensione*. We filled the bath with the hottest water possible and Lisle got in. I perched on the side of the bath and Gertie sat on the toilet. We each took a copious mouthful of vodka to give Lisle encouragement. We continued encouraging her as we passed the bottle between us and until even Lisle grew very merry. We finally went to bed and slept very late.

Lisle was the first to wake. "It didn't work."

The situation was desperate and we had terrible hangovers to boot.

The optimistic Gertie came up with another solution. "Do you remember the gentleman who sent me flowers the other night? It said on his card he was a doctor. I will accept his invitation tonight and the three of us will go and meet him."

That night, an attractive middle-aged Italian, a little like Rossano Brazzi, was waiting for Gertie in a two-seater sports car.

"Hello," three voices called out at the same time.

It was hard to tell whether he was disappointed or couldn't believe his luck. He got out of the car and we three squeezed in. We just left enough room for him to drive. Because of the war, most Italians spoke a little German and we explained that we never moved without each other. We had had to make a promise to our parents – otherwise they would not have let us go on the tour. He drove us to a typical Italian trattoria and after several glasses of cold sparkling Italian wine, Gertie, his favourite, told him of our predicament.

"You see, we are pregnant, and we need to get unpregnant."

"All of you are pregnant?"

I think he thought it was a joke. Three girls pregnant at the same time was rather unusual.

"No, but as ladies, we will not reveal which one of us is in the predicament."

Any hopes the poor man may have had for a romantic evening alone with Gertie had long disappeared. He promised to think about it and would see us again the following evening.

He duly arrived with another attractive middle-aged man as reinforcement. Lisle and I got into his car whilst Gertie travelled with her doctor. We ended up at the same trattoria. The meal was almost over and the doctor, although making no attempt to hide his feelings for Gertie, had made no mention of our predicament. I was getting very agitated but Lisle didn't show the slightest anxiety. We three girls met up in the toilet.

"Gertie, you must do something," I demanded.

"Why me?"

"You're the one he likes. You must do it tonight."

The other man dropped Lisle and I off at the *pensione,* where we sat up anxiously waiting for Gertie. She returned an hour or so later with her hard-earned prize: a sterilized syringe and a kidney-shaped dish. It looked very alarming to me, but Lisle, a doctor's daughter, took it in very calmly. My estimation of Gertie had gone up 100%.

"The doctor was very understanding once I had explained the whole situation."

"What next?" I asked.

"Lisle must lie on the bed with her bottom up. It will be difficult to get the needle in, but the injection should do it."

"Gertie, I can't watch," I said. "I will be completely useless. I can't stand seeing blood or needles."

"You'll have to, Dora; hold Lisle's hands."

Lisle was already on the bed with her bare bottom awaiting puncture. I held her hands, but as soon as I saw the needle of Gertie's syringe, I felt giddy. When the needle was about to prick Lisle's bottom I screamed in agony, causing the point to jump back again. I couldn't believe how patiently Lisle lay there, not saying a word. Gertie tried again but the needle wouldn't penetrate the skin. I tried not to look.

"Dora, stop squeezing up your face. You're not a help at all."

"Gertie, I'm holding Lisle's hands."

Gertie made another unsuccessful attempt. Who would have thought that Lisle's skin was that tough? Gertie decided to push it in with more force from a distance. It just bounced back at her. Even Gertie's optimism had its limits.

"Lisle, I'm sorry. I can't do it. We'll just have to wait until we get back to Vienna."

The management organising the tour was a very dubious one. Money was never paid on time and never in full. Several members of the company had had enough and quit in Genoa. We decided to stay, I had always wanted to see Sicily, *Cavalleria Rusticana* was my favourite opera, and so we went on with the depleted show to Catania – bits were cut out or the remaining singers sang extra songs. Catania still bore the scars of the Allied invasion of 1943. The atmosphere was much harsher and slightly menacing. In Italy, the men would smile and whistle, but in Sicily they wouldn't leave us alone. They became angry when we didn't react and would spit at us in the street. They would glare at us with their hard eyes; they looked so sinister that we were afraid to go to the beach. We were becoming very bored and homesick and were therefore pleased to find an invitation for dinner with the Mayor of Catania waiting for us at the theatre. We accepted at once. There was nothing to be afraid of: it was an official dinner after the final performance. A taxi was waiting at the stage door and the three of us, dressed in the only cocktail dresses we had brought with us, stepped into it and the chauffeur drove away. It was only then that we realised that we were the only ones who had received an invitation from the Mayor. After a short while we noticed that we had driven out of the city into the dark countryside.

"Where is the dinner party?"

"At his Excellency's villa."

That must be alright, we thought, and relaxed. We arrived at some big gates which closed behind us as we drove through, and continued up a long and dark drive. The car's headlamps lit up a long two-storied building. Light blazed from the French windows which lined the entire ground floor. We got out of the taxi, which drove away immediately, and walked up some stairs into a room where men were seated at a long table laid out for dinner. There were only men, not a single woman. Their leered at us as if they were anticipating a particularly juicy steak. Our faces were fixed with disbelief as we were seated close to the mayor. He gave a signal and some servants went to the windows and closed the shutters. We were like three birds trapped in a cage. We looked at each other before Gertie made a decision.

"When I get up, we all run out into the garden. Hold hands."

We got up and ran, but we didn't get very far. The shutters were firmly closed. We turned together and faced the astonished faces looking at us from the table.

"We want to go back to our hotel!" We screamed in unison.

"My father holds a very important government position – you won't get away with it!" added Lisle.

I'm sure the Mayor didn't care what position Lisle's father held, but he obviously realised that he had invited the wrong sort of girls. He was angry and disappointed.

"Why don't you have some wine and eat something? Then I will have you driven you back."

We were petrified. Eat? Drink? Who knows what they had put in the food? Drinking was out of the question. We went back to the table and just sat and nibbled on a few grapes, holding hands tightly, waiting to be taken home. Nobody touched us, but the Mayor deliberately made us wait until they had finished the final course of their very long meal. He was clearly a man who didn't like not having things his own way: he had expected a little fun and action with some easy girls. He glared at us malevolently as the taxi finally drove us away.

We were very frightened and locked the shutters of our room when we got back to our *pensione* even though it was an extremely hot night and the fan wasn't working. We hardly slept and decided to leave Sicily first thing in the morning. We quickly packed and went down stairs to find the company manager to get the remaining money we were owed, but found to our consternation that he had run off with the money during the night. We had been stranded.

Gertie voiced our thoughts. "Let's get the Hell out of here."

We didn't want to wait for a bus or train to take us to the ferry. Besides, the Mayor might have associates at the railway station or port who could make things difficult for us. The quickest way home was flying and although none of us had flown before, we decided that there was nothing for it but to get to the airport at Messina and get the first flight out, no matter where it went. We ordered a taxi but when it arrived the driver looked very like the one who had driven us to the Mayor's house the previous night. We were still in shock. Had he been sent by the Mayor? Where was he going to take us? Our eyes didn't leave to the road signs, making sure we were heading to Messina. He left the main road once and we all three jumped up in panic.

"Stop the car!"

He stopped and explained it was a short cut. We insisted on seeing the map. We never relaxed until we drove into the airport. The first flight was an Alitalia to Milan. We checked our money. It was just enough. It was only when we were sitting in the departure lounge with our tickets grasped firmly in our hands that Gertie felt safe enough to open her mouth.

"You both realise that the Mayor and his friends were *mafiosi*."

We most certainly did. We were all so tense, that we hardly experienced any excitement when we left the ground on our first flight. Milan felt like being in a civilised country again. Lisle phoned her parents, who arranged for her and me to get train tickets to Vienna. Gertie phoned a so-called 'rich uncle', who came and picked her up.

Lisle had no choice but to tell her parents of her predicament. They were very understanding. Arrangements were made, and the predicament was never mentioned among us again.

16

1957

An exciting new season opened with *Kiss Me Kate,* the first-ever production of an American musical at the Volksoper. Heinz Rosen, a modern choreographer, was brought over from Munich with his solo dancer, and Olive Moorefield and Hubert Dilworth arrived from Broadway. They were both black and caused quite a stir. Apart from American servicemen, a black face was then a great rarity in Vienna. I was intrigued by Heinz Rosen's new style of dancing, moving to the rhythm with loose hips and arms. It was free, packed with vitality and excitement and, although I wasn't in the show, I watched every rehearsal I could, particularly those of the big dance number, *Too Damn'd Hot.* The scene was supposed to be backstage in a theatre and two piles of packing cases had been arranged to make high podiums. Hubert, who was a great jazz singer, sang on top of one, whilst the dancer from Munich danced on the other; faster and faster with each succeeding chorus, eventually flying backwards into the air to be caught by members of the male *corps de ballet* beneath. It was the highlight of the show, which became the biggest success in the history of the Volksoper and would continue in the repertoire for many years. After a few performances the dancer strained a ligament and, having seen me watching so many rehearsals, Heinz Rosen asked me to take over her part – Hattie, Katerina's dresser. I accepted eagerly, wanting to master this new technique and sensing the possibilities. I had no idea then how it would eventually change the entire course of my life. I threw myself into it with my usual determination; at first I felt awkward, my movements were too balletic, but I worked and practiced and gradually improved with every performance.

The only problem was that the part required that I spoke a couple of lines. I was more nervous of those two lines than all the solo dancing scenes put together. The star of the show, Fred Leever, was a classical actor from the Burgtheater. He was in his forties, handsome in the Clark Gable manner, and had a similar reputation with the ladies to that of Ferry Windberger. There was always a crowd of girls clamouring for his autograph at the stage door. He noticed how nervous I was and took pity on me, offering to help me with my two lines. He began to watch me each night and give me encouragement from the wings. When he was offstage we would sit and talk, and as ever I was eager to learn from another font of wisdom, at the same time voicing my own opinions.

"Dora, you see everything in black and white. There are many shades in between."

"How can it be? There is only right and wrong."

"Don't judge anyone if you haven't been there yourself. Stay quiet, and the years will teach you."

Carlos had finally disappeared from my life and I was gradually retreating from the overpowering attentions of Dudi. Fred took me to quiet little *gasthauses* after the show, to the great envy of all the girls at the stage door, but we never stayed out late. He was a busy actor, making films during the day, and usually had to get up early.

I also became friendly with Olive Moorefield, who was only a few years older than me. She was very vibrant and very beautiful. She had not had an easy life, being born into a family with seven brothers and sisters in the steel town of Pittsburgh, Pennsylvania. She had worked her way through college, taking singing and acting lessons, and had broken into Broadway by sheer guts and determination. She was well-skilled in getting what she wanted and I admired her for it. She began by playing Bianca but soon took over the leading role of Katherina, opposite Fred Leever. She became quite a celebrity and was constantly being invited to sing at gala evenings and events. She would often take me to her apartment and I was in seventh heaven going through her wardrobe; I had never imagined that anyone could have so many clothes. She had a room filled with the most exquisitely styled evening gowns with matching accessories and would parade before me and Ron, her very large black poodle complete with his diamond-studded collar. Ron and I enjoyed a private fashion show until she finally decided what to wear for that particular night. Sometimes it took several hours. She had made herself very sophisticated and had great taste, but was also very generous. She would let me try on any gown or dress I particularly admired and if it suited me would occasionally make me a present.

I went with her and Hubert to cocktail parties at

their Embassy and got to know their generous but endearingly naive fellow-countrymen. Thanks to the movies, we imagined everybody in America was rich and everything was efficient and ultra-modern; even Coco-Cola in its distinctive bottle was considered chic and so sophisticated. Apart from gangsters like James Cagney and Humphrey Bogart, Americans lived in an enchanted world of peace and comfort. When they invited me to their luxurious homes on the outskirts of Vienna, fitted with all the latest devices such as washing machines and refrigerators, then virtually unknown to most Europeans, with big, shining American limousines parked on the drive, I began to believe it was true. On top of that they fed me to bursting with giant steaks, lashings of ice cream in flavours I'd never believed possible, and bananas, oranges, chocolates – in quantities I'd hardly ever seen in restaurants, let alone in private homes.

The Cold War was in full flow and the Embassy was in the thick of it. Austria was perched on the eastern extremity of what was then considered the free world – people disappeared, spies were supposedly constantly crossing the border in both directions. One evening, Olive introduced me to good-looking, dark haired man in his mid-thirties.

"Dora, Max Weiss, has just joined the Embassy and would like to meet you."

I put out my hand and saw to my embarrassment that his right arm was missing.

He smiled charmingly, "Don't worry. People do that all the time. I lost it in the war."

He asked me where I was from and became very interested when I said Bulgaria.

"You've got to tell me all about it. Let me take you to dinner."

I followed him outside and was a little concerned when he got behind the wheel of an open sports car. He was very perceptive.

"It's OK. I can do most things better with one hand than other men do with two."

He drove with great speed and no little skill to his apartment on the other side of town.

"We'll have more privacy here than in a restaurant," he said, as he lit candles before opening a bottle of French wine and pouring me a glass.

"Do you want me to help you cook?"

"Leave everything to me."

And I did, with great relief as I didn't have the faintest idea how to cook at that time. I sat and drank exquisite white wine whilst he prepared steaks and salad. He wanted to know how I came out of Bulgaria, what route I had taken, and if I had any contacts there. All my family had gone, as had practically all of the Jews we had known; I couldn't tell him very much, but he noted down everything I did tell him very carefully. I began to wonder if he was a spy, working for the CIA, or whatever it was called then. But he could hardly go undercover with one arm – there couldn't be many one-armed spies in the world. Nevertheless he was very charming, and after dinner drove me home quite safely with his one arm.

Hardy didn't see any future for himself in Vienna and had taken a job managing a bar for American soldiers in Wurzburg, Germany. I missed my brother and having a few days off decided to visit him. I had seen lots of American musicals about the army and thought it would be quite an exciting place. I could not have been more wrong. There was nothing glamourous about it – no trace of Vera Ellen or Cyd Charisse dancing at the Stage Door Canteen. Hardy's bar was simply a one story prefabricated building in what had once been a garden between two houses, with simple wooden tables and chairs and walls cluttered with peeling posters of half-naked girls or seashores with palm trees and sunshine. The place, I suppose not unnaturally, reeked of beer. Hardy was serving behind the bar.

"Hardy, what on earth are you doing here?"

"Making money."

He couldn't get away so I stayed with him throughout the evening. A jukebox constantly blared out music, but there were no women to dance with. Some hard-faced women were kept firmly outside by the 'snowdrops' – the white-helmeted military police. By ten o'clock the place was packed with big, noisy, boisterous men. Hardy kept me safely behind the bar. He worked so hard. I realised how lucky I was doing something that I loved. He had no choice. He was still serving beer when I left and remained until the bar closed in the early hours of the morning. He obviously had no time for me. I went back to Vienna the same day.

The entire opera was awaiting the arrival of a young genius from Czechoslovakia, Dalibor Brazda, to conduct Janacek's *Der Schlaue Fuchslein (Cunning Little Vixen)*. Brazda was still conducting *Porgy and Bess* in New York and rehearsals began without him. Czechoslovakia was behind the Iron Curtain and we were surprised that he was allowed to travel so freely. Dia Luca was choreographer and gave me an excellent part; the only problem was that I had to sing a few lines before I started to dance. Speaking lines was one thing but singing them was quite another. Not even Fred Leever could help me with that. After several agonising sessions with the choirmaster, the decision was unanimous:

"Dora will mime her words and a singer back stage will sing for her."

My relief was unbounded. Brazda eventually arrived, dark-haired, lively and very handsome, with a red scarf tied around his neck, and all the different elements of the production: ballet, chorus, solo singers and orchestra were brought together for a dress rehearsal. I was supposed to be a small animal lying on an imaginary tree stump. I heard my cue, picked up my head, looked left and right and then straight at Brazda, his baton went down, I opened my mouth, and a fearful noise came from behind me. I looked back into the wings and beheld a huge woman, five times my size, with a voice so powerful that it would have been heard on the far side of the Danube.

"Lights!" The baton crashed down on the podium.

"Who is singing? I can't have a little body up there

with the voice of a giant." He turned his attention to me. "You, do you know the words?"

I nodded my head although the rest of me was shaking.

"Good. Then you sing it."

An orchestra, nearly fifty strong and he was asking me to sing?

His baton came down, the orchestra came crashing in and my voice was drowned without a trace. The baton crashed on the podium once more.

"Try again." He said matter-of-factly.

His baton waved gently and the orchestra played pianissimo, pianissimo.

"That's a little better. Choirmaster! Practice with her. Teach her to sing!"

The poor man looked at me in desperation. The lights went down and Brazda continued with his rehearsal. When I had finished my dance I went into the auditorium to watch. He didn't conduct like the other conductors I had seen. He let the orchestra go wild, then drew them back, before releasing them again even more freely, he stopped and reprimanded and sang, bursting with emotion and love of music. The orchestra played better than I'd ever heard them before. By the end of the day everybody realised why he had become a maestro so young.

I worked hard with the choirmaster and in a few days I was coping with the singing a little better. Brazda stopped the orchestra during my dance.

"How is the tempo? If you feel comfortable during

the arabesque, hold the balance longer and I will take the music with you."

His baton wove patterns through the air and it was if he was holding back the orchestra for me. He was dancing with me, we were almost breathing together.

The rehearsals continued for several weeks and we studied each other, becoming closer and closer. We both came from the same background; he too had suffered in the war and had struggled so hard to achieve his dreams. One evening, after rehearsal, I went back with him to his room, in an apartment which he said belonged to friends. It was very small, almost a cell, with room only for a bed with a shelf of books above it, and a portable gramophone; the window looked out into the dark well of the building. We sat on the bed. He took off his red scarf, then his shirt. My dress slipped off me. He leant his face close to mine. I could feel his breath on my cheek before he touched my breast. Everything seemed right and natural. It was if we were dancing together. He had watched me so much that he knew my body better than I did myself. We clung to each other afterwards, like two shipwrecked children who had survived a stormy sea.

We became inseparable, everyone accepted our togetherness. We had lunch together every day at the same table in the coffee house opposite the stage door. I danced, he conducted. I never missed a chance of watching him rehearse with the orchestra, and on the evenings I danced in other shows, he would watch me from the audience. Sometimes, he would come into the practice room and take over the piano during our training classes. He played with such feeling and gusto that we could not but help being better dancers. All the girls loved him but I loved him most. Life could not get any better. But it did. I received a letter from Schwartz, the leading agent in Vienna, informing me that John Cranko, the renowned and innovative director and choreographer, had been travelling all over Europe, choosing dancers that he thought would be suitable for the brand new ballet company he was forming in Stuttgart. Cranko had seen me dance and wanted me as a coryphée. I was the only one he wanted out of the entire company. I couldn't believe it. It was everything I had ever wished. I discussed it with Brazda – I always called him 'Brazda' never Dalibor, Brazda suited him better – and we both agreed that I should accept. I was only eighteen, I had a long way to go, but in a year or two I could be a solo dancer in one of the most exciting companies in Europe. Brazda would easily find a position in Germany; he wouldn't have any problem with his qualifications, he had already received an offer from the Munich Opera. We would go to Germany together at the end of the season: a new life – a new beginning together. We were full of hope and dreams and ambitions. And we were madly and passionately in love.

On the evenings we were both free, we went to concerts and would always end up in his little cell-like room, where he would play his gramophone and make me listen to the same scores played by different conductors. He taught me to recognise the nuances and alternative interpretations. The one thing I could not understand was why I never saw or heard the owners of the flat. I had only been in his little room.

"Brazda, shall I bring your friends flowers?" I asked on one occasion. "It would be nice to meet them."

He stiffened at once and shook his head.

I began to see that something was troubling him. I didn't know what it was. I didn't want to spoil our happiness, but finally, one afternoon, I forced myself to ask him.

"Dora, I'm being watched. They want to know when I will be returning to Prague."

"Tell them you won't go back. You are going to Germany."

"No, we mustn't antagonise them. They know about you and they want me to go back for Christmas."

"Brazda, if you go you will never come back."

He took me in his arms; Tchaikovsky was playing softly on the gramophone. We sat down on that little bed as he held my face and looked deep into my eyes.

"Dora, I'm frightened. My mother is there, they can make me go back. You know they can."

I remembered the terrible stories of what had just happened in Hungary, and knew it was true. That night we clung on to each other, tighter than ever, as if each was afraid of losing the other. As we made love, he cried.

"I will never leave you," he promised, early next morning as I went to practice.

He didn't come to the coffee house at lunch time. He didn't watch my rehearsal. There was no note, no message, nothing. That evening there was no sign of him at the theatre. The performance was delayed for more than half an hour. The other dancers chatted unconcerned in the wings, whilst I desperately scoured the orchestra pit through the peep hole in the curtain. Surely he would come? He had to come. My heart fell when eventually the house conductor took over the podium. The music was familiar but I was dancing in a different ballet. My tears caught in the lights as I jerked my head. The performance never seemed to end. When it did, I changed quickly and ran to the apartment and rang the bell frantically

The door was opened by a non-descript looking man.

"Is Brazda here?"

"No. What do you want?"

"I'm his friend. I want to see him."

I pushed past him and went into the first door on the left, into that familiar little room. The bed was neatly made. There was no trace of the fervent love we had so recently made upon it. His records were piled up on the small table next to his gramophone. His books were still on the shelf. He had so few possessions for such a great talent, and he had lost even these. It was worse than a nightmare. The man had followed me into Brazda's room. I realised then that he had been his jailer. I ran past him, out of that apartment back to the only person who could comfort me.

"Mama, Brazda has gone."

Nevertheless, every night the Janacek was performed,

I went down to the peephole to watch the podium in case he came back. He never did.

Many years later I met Heidi in London when she came to dance at the Festival Hall. She always seemed to bring sad tidings.

"Brazda came back, Dora. You would not have recognised him. He had been two years in the Gulags and the only way he survived was by drinking vodka. He was in Vienna playing the piano for a small folk dancing group. As soon as he arrived he came looking for you – all I could tell him was that you were in London, but I didn't know where."

All my grief for him returned. God, how could they do that to my Brazda? Was it only because of our love? But I knew such a talent could not be extinguished.

I only found out after his death in 2005, that Dalibor Brazda eventually made it to the West. He settled in Germany and had a very successful musical career before he died in Switzerland. He never married.

17

Travels with Ron

The pain of losing Brazda never left me. I did everything I could to help me forget, but was desperate for his love. When Olive went away on an engagement for a few days, I volunteered to look after her poodle Ron, who had become very fond of me. So Mama, I, and a great black dog were crammed into the one and a half rooms. It would have been far from comfortable at the best of times, but was worse because I had no performances or rehearsals that week and did not feel like going out. Mama could see how I was suffering.

"Dorale, why don't you use the air ticket that your cousin Bernie sent you? Go and visit him in Geneva. A change of scenery will do you good."

"But I promised Olive I would take care of Ron."

"Take him with you." Mama liked animals but not in her home.

"To Geneva?"

"Yes."

"But I have no money."

"Don't worry, Bernie will take care of you. He is your cousin."

It sounded a good idea. Bernie had quickly become very, very rich, as he had said he would. He reputedly lived in a huge penthouse in the centre of Geneva. A picture formed in my mind. Flying on an aeroplane with a big black poodle with matching diamond studded collar and lead was certainly glamourous. I would be like my favourite film star Audrey Hepburn, even if Ron's diamonds were only imitation. I phoned Bernie's office, left a message that I was coming, put on a copy of a blue Chanel suit that the wardrobe department had made for me, and took a taxi to the airport.

The airport still bore the signs of the heavy bombing in the war. The terminal was nothing more than a large prefabricated hut. I had no trouble getting Ron on the plane but had not expected that he would need a ticket, which cost me most of the money I had with me. Ron and I walked out of the terminal on to the tarmac and mounted the steps into the plane with all eyes upon us. He was very calm, giving the impression that he was obviously very used to flying, and on boarding climbed up on the seat next to me as if it was the most natural thing in the world. I apologised to him that we were not travelling First Class.

Things were more like Ron was used to when we landed in Geneva in the late afternoon, where Bernie's chauffeur-driven Bentley was awaiting to convey us to his offices in a big modern building in the Rue de Lausanne. Bernie's company IOS (Investors Overseas Services) occupied the entire top floor. I held Ron in one hand and my suitcase in the other and took the lift up to the reception area. Everything was new and modern: big low glass tables, strewn the latest editions of *Time, Life,*

Newsweek and other American Magazines, and huge, comfortable sofas that you could literally sink into. The walls were covered with financial charts and graphs that didn't make any sense to me. Smart young Americans in button-down shirts and well-cut light trousers were moving busily from room to room. Attractive secretaries were typing frantically away. I asked for Mr Cornfeld and a pretty young lady directed me to a door at the end of a long corridor. I knocked and Bernie opened it. He seemed a little surprised to see me. I rather think he had forgotten I was coming

"Oh! Hi, Dora."

Ron gave a friendly bark.

"Who is that?"

"Ron."

He seemed more pleased to see Ron than me and started to play with him. They got on very well together. Bernie gave me a cousinly kiss and asked me to wait. I sat on a black leather sofa, while Ron chose to lie most stylishly on a white fluffy rug by my feet. Bernie went to an over-sized desk, behind which was an entire wall of glass, and pulled out a drawer that looked like a table with buttons. He began pushing them and made telephone calls at the same time. I sat quietly and gazed over Bernie's head through the glass wall to the park and the lake beyond, remembering my time with Ferry – the morning in a little boat, the water around us sparkling in the sun, me swivelling around in my full skirt and petticoat, while he photographed me from every angle. I saw it all – my blue skirt with a spider's web print, white blouse, flat ballerina shoes and white socks – it was like watching another Dora I once knew, a sixteen-year old girl with her first love. Mama said, 'What comes goes. Don't look back, go forward.' I was trying so hard to do just that – I had achieved so much in that short time. I was now a solo dancer in the Volksoper, with as many admirers as I could wish, but I couldn't help myself longing for the other Dora.

"Dora, let's go."

I was startled out of my reverie.

"Yes."

I followed Bernie to the lift, carrying my suitcase and holding Ron tightly on his leash. We took the lift to the ground floor where Bernie opened the door of a very small room, with a bed, a sink, a small table and two uncomfortable looking chairs.

"Dora, you will stay here. There's a rest room with a shower down the corridor. Do what you like during the day and in the evenings we will go out together."

It wasn't what I had expected, but I had become all too used to small dark rooms. I left my suitcase there, took Ron and followed Bernie out to his car – not the Bentley but open American sports car – I couldn't recognise the make.

"We are going to my apartment to pick up my girlfriend; then we will have dinner with some friends in a restaurant."

His apartment was also on the top floor of a newly-built block, with windows on every side overlooking all of Geneva. There were luxurious furnishings, even a huge illuminated fish tank, bigger than anything I'd ever seen before, but everything seemed to be in chaos with books and newspapers scattered all over the place. The bedroom door was open and I could see expensive dresses and gowns strewn across an unmade bed. Many still had labels on them.

Bernie's current girlfriend, Françoise, was waiting for him along with two multi-coloured cats, who seemed even less pleased to meet Ron than Monique was to meet me. She began a one-sided dialogue with Bernie in French. In between her taking breaths, Bernie managed the odd "*Oui,*" or would smile and nod his head, before dipping his hand into his pocket and carelessly giving her what looked like a large quantity of dollar bills. I thought they were very ill-matched, she wasn't even attractive, with a hard face and thin mousey hair, but she must have been giving Bernie something he wanted.

We drove to a restaurant, with Ron and I squeezed into the buggy seat in the rear, where some people were already eating. Bernie introduced me as his little cousin, the ballet dancer, and we sat down to dinner. Ron crept under the table; he was even hungrier than me. Bernie's friends were ordering their dessert before we had ordered our entrée – but in fact we didn't order anything. Françoise took it upon herself to order for us. She decided upon some heavy meat dish, which I suspected was pork. I passed most of mine under the table to a very grateful Ron. Bernie didn't seem to notice or mind. He looked very tired as he told jokes in a very soft voice. He always spoke softly, as if it were too much of an effort for him to speak any louder. You had to constantly strain to catch the gist of what he was saying. Nevertheless, his friends laughed dutifully at every joke, although I could not understand half of them. It was very late when we left the restaurant and Bernie dropped me and Ron off at our very meagre lodging in Rue de Lausanne.

I awoke in the morning with Ron on top of me, fast asleep. He must have known I was lonely. I washed in the sink, showered in the toilet along the corridor, dressed and walked out into the rich and comfortable atmosphere of Rue Lausanne, where smartly dressed bankers and their secretaries were hurrying to their offices and desks. There was something very smug and satisfied about them. I suspect that they wouldn't have cared who had won the war as long as their bank vaults remained full. I crossed the road and took Ron into the park for his morning necessities. Ron led me down to the lake, to a lovely restaurant, *La Perle du Lac,* where people were enjoying a delicious breakfast by the water's edge. Ron's stomach must have been rumbling like mine, but I knew I couldn't afford breakfast there. But Ron didn't know that – he just wanted breakfast. I counted the money in my little purse and took him to a nearby bakery where we shared two croissants.

Something had gone very wrong. I had imagined we would be staying in Bernie's apartment, where we would have been fed. I wasn't so much worried for myself, I had become used to being hungry one way or another over the years, but I had a responsibility to Ron. He was used to the very best. I could have asked Bernie for money, he could certainly afford it, but my pride wouldn't allow it. I didn't want to be a taker like Francoise, even if I was Bernie's cousin.

I looked at Ron, who was gazing up at me devotedly and wagging his tail.

"My father told me that nobody can look inside your stomach – you'll have just one meal a day here and it will be in the evenings. Come on; let's have a look at the United Nations."

We found the *Palais des Nations*, a beautiful art deco building in a peaceful park. The flags of all the nations were fluttering in two long lines outside. I was very moved to see the Star of David amongst them and recalled Kurtie's words at that Gordonia-Maccabi camp years before: "What happened to the Jewish people in the years of Hitler must never be repeated. We will never allow ourselves to be led again like cattle into the slaughterhouse. We will fight for our freedom and Israel, our own country."

The motto over the entrance: *People of the World United* didn't appear to be doing much good; the world was divided into two camps: NATO and the Warsaw Pact. The wartime allies, Russia and America, Communism and Capitalism, were striving for domination. Everything was a mess, but at least we Jews now had somewhere to run to.

I wandered into the old town; it still felt strange being in a city that had not been damaged in the war. Many of the buildings were beautiful and the shops were luxurious and expensive. I enjoyed looking at their windows even though I couldn't afford a single thing. I left Ron alone for a while in the afternoon to visit the huge *Musee d'Art de d'Histoire,* luckily admission was free. I gazed at the paintings of Rembrandt, Cezanne and Modigliani and remembered all that Ferry had taught me. That would never be taken away.

I wandered back at four having bought Ron another croissant as a reward for being good, and promised him it would soon be time to eat a proper meal. I took another shower, dressed and lay on the bed waiting for Bernie to come down and pick us up. I was still lying on the bed at eight. Ron was looking at me, imploringly.

"I know Ron. You are right. It's time for food. Wait here, I will go upstairs and see where Bernie is."

I found my cousin rapt on the telephone, oblivious to everything around him. He eventually finished and looked up at me with great surprise.

"Oh, Dora. I won't be long."

"OK. I'll wait downstairs."

I knew he had forgotten all about me. He was totally absorbed by his work. I didn't know what he was doing, but he was certainly totally absorbed. Ten o'clock passed. I had never waited for anyone but now I had no choice. At midnight I could stand it no longer. If this was Bernie's routine for dinner dates it was not for me. I went up again this time with Ron. Bernie was just putting down the phone.

"Hi, Dora. Good that you came up. We're going."

Ron wagged his tail in joyful expectation.

Bernie noticed him for the first time. "Sorry, we

can't take him. We're going to *Griffin's*. They don't allow dogs."

By now I had had enough. "But Bernie, the poor dog is starving. He hasn't eaten all day."

Bernie gave his lazy smile. "No problem, we'll bring him back a doggy bag."

A doggy bag? It was an American expression then unknown to me. I would use it a lot for feeding myself over the coming years. I reluctantly returned Ron to our little room. He looked sad and I felt sad too.

I was still angry with Bernie. "Why do you have to work so late?" I demanded as I got into his car.

"I always work late because of the time difference between Europe and the US. I have to be in control until the markets close."

Bernie was charming for the rest of the night, evening had long gone. *Griffins*, was an ultra-expensive nightclub which definitely put the tawdry clubs of Vienna to shame. Everything was in red and black, the ornately decorated columns, the low-slung leather banquettes, the illuminated dance floor. The walls were hung with huge paintings and large exotic plants were growing everywhere. Françoise was already there with other acquaintances, all of whom looked very rich and very spoilt. The atmosphere was unrestrained flirtation – people constantly came and left our table – there was none of the formality of Vienna. There was a discotheque, the first I had ever seen, and Bernie asked me to dance. I hoped that he was a better financier than dancer – his movements were awkward – but I enjoyed it far more than sitting with his so-called friends. The food was excellent and this time I ordered a large steak. Bernie had a word with the waiter and I discovered what a doggy bag was when he came back with a huge package of left-over meat.

It was four in the morning when Bernie dropped me back at Rue Lausanne. I gave him a goodnight kiss on his cheek and hurried to Ron to present him with the feast of his life.

Every day I expected Bernie to ask me if I needed any money, but he never did. I was determined not to ask him for a penny. I refused to put myself on the same level as Françoise and the other takers. Ron and I developed a routine: long walk and croissants in the morning, art gallery visits for me in the afternoon, late night restaurants with Bernie, and early morning doggy bag feasts for Ron. One night we dined in a strip club which was definitely not to my taste, although Ron, who was allowed to come with us that time, did not seem to mind. The routine was broken one day when Bernie drove me across the border into France to visit an American couple who were living in an old chateau they were slowly restoring. I was astounded when Bernie informed me he was thinking of doing the same thing. He had money to throw around like confetti and we were so poor. Perhaps Hardy should work for him. It would definitely be better than that awful bar in Germany. After five days I was happy to return to my more humble existence, so was Ron. I had managed to survive on my money although Mama had to pay for the taxi when we arrived home.

18

Hungarian Rhapsody

I went back to my regimented life at the ballet, which totally absorbed me. It was my escape from reality, and gave me purpose and security. I was never short of admirers but I didn't need men. I always had Mama, who showered me with undemanding and unselfish love. Papa was still working at his soul-destroying job in the *gasthaus*, but whenever he visited he somehow managed to make his blue eyes sparkle with humour, and Gertie and Lisle were always faithful to me.

An American admirer of Gertie had invited her for a drink in the Blue Bar at the Hotel Sacher. She had so many friends and admirers I had no idea how she found the time to meet them all.

"Dora, do you want to come along? It's before the performance but we are only doing *Nabucco*. We don't have much to do in it."

It was true. All we had to do was share a little solo together. I accepted.

The Blue Bar, furnished in magnificent shades of blue brocaded silk, was definitely the place to be. It was small and intimate, set in the very heart of the hotel, and reputedly frequented by both American and Russian spies.

Gertie's American, whose name was Rick, was big and friendly, as nearly all of them were: "You must have a martini. George makes the best martini in Europe."

"Why not?" we said, giving the impression we were used to them although neither of us had tried one before. We settled into the lushly upholstered couches and sipped out of the distinctive glasses like two stars in a Hollywood film. We both liked the taste, especially the olive as we were quite hungry. Rick was entertaining and a perfect host and ordered two more. While we were drinking them, a man came into the bar with two blonde-haired young women.

Rick beckoned him over. "Ladies, may I introduce Stefan Watzik – we met here in the bar last night."

Stefan was in his thirties, very attractive, almost beautiful, but in a manly way. Gertie and I stretched our hands towards him, which he duly kissed in a gentlemanly manner.

"May we join you?" He had a strong Hungarian accent. He sat down with his ladies, although I could tell they were not ladies. They were displaying their considerable bosoms in low-cut decolletes, and one should never put one's hand on a man's knee in public.

Rick ordered another round of drinks whilst the newcomer talked. I realised at once that he was not my type. He talked too much, telling one joke after another. He was flamboyant, confident of his sex appeal, constantly trying to make an impression. I was eating my third olive and feeling rather bored, when I casually glanced at my watch.

"My God, Gertie! Look at the time! We have to get to the theatre!"

We jumped up, thanked Rick and made a quick exit. We ran through the small lobby out into the fresh air with the huge mass of the bomb-damaged Staatstoper before us. The only problem was both of us saw it double.

"Gertie, my head is spinning round and round!"

"Dora, mine too."

The martinis had been easy to drink but they had had a devastating effect – and all for three little olives.

"I will never touch that drink again. How on earth will we manage to dance?" I was almost in tears. Being late for a performance was unthinkable in the ballet, but being late and tipsy was considerably more than unthinkable.

"Dora, a cold shower will help." Gertie could always be trusted to come up with a solution.

We took a taxi to the Volksoper where my ever-malevolent dresser was waiting.

"What on earth do you think you are doing? I should report you. The performance has already started. You deserve expulsion. " She sounded even more like a Nazi than usual.

We ran straight into the cold shower. The dresser dressed me and the hairdresser put on my wig whilst I hastily applied my make-up. My eye lines were rather crooked that night. We could hear the music coming towards our cue. We ran down to the stage. Thank God we were Hebrew slaves dancing in bare feet – I would not have been able to balance on my toes for the world.

The dance was just a haze. Gertie simply followed my steps, as she usually did, but I had no idea if they were correct, although the audience didn't seem to notice. We staggered off and sobered up with cups of Dudi Deutsch's strongest black coffee.

"Gertie, I will never go out with you before a performance again," I hissed as we went out through the stage door.

"There you are at last. You're coming out with us." It was Rick and Stefan and the two girls, in extremely high spirits

Gertie and I looked at each other. All the tension left us and we burst out laughing. They had been drinking away all evening whilst we had been scared to death, struggling to sober up and perform. There was nothing we could do but fall in with their carefree mood and let them whisk us off to the *heurigen*, the wine taverns in Grinzing. We must have made a striking group – wherever we went the women looked at Stefan and the men at Gertie, but Stefan ignored all the other women, including his two ladies, and directed his attention entirely on me. I did nothing to encourage him but smile at his jokes. Stefan then insisted he wanted to dance with me, and took us all on to the Trummelhof – at that time the most fashionable place in all of Vienna. We danced to romantic songs which he sang softly in my ear and held me so tight to his big, manly chest that my feet were swept up off the floor. I didn't have to move my legs. We were all still dancing and very happy when we took to the street. We stopped at a *wurst* stand where Gertie and I finally staved off our ravenous hunger with tasty smoked *krakauers*, before piling into a taxi, sitting on top of each other, to the dismay of the poor driver.

I was the first to be dropped off. I said 'Goodnight', but 'Good morning' would have been far more appropriate.

I liked challenging my body and a night without sleep was no problem for me. I showered and went to practise. Nevertheless, after the performance that night I was looking forward to a peaceful time with Mama at home.

"Hello, Dora. I've bought along an old friend who wanted to meet you."

The Hungarian Hercules was back at the stage door with the two girls and another man.

"Dora, isn't it a coincidence – Stefan was telling me about this beautiful young dancer he had met and I realised it was you,"

It was Kurtie, my old leader at the Gordonia, hugging me warmly. I realised for the first time that my blonde Hungarian was Jewish.

"Come, we must celebrate your reunion." Stefan was already hailing a taxi.

"It must be a short celebration. I am tired."

We went to several bars and wherever we went Stefan picked up the bill as he had done the night before. I managed to find out more about him. He had come out of Hungary several years before the revolution and had built a successful business in Germany which often brought him to Vienna. He never told me what his business was, but I didn't ponder on it. Nobody asked too many questions then. People didn't want to know about the past or where you came from. They lived for the present moment and all the fun that went with it. Stefan insisted that I tried Hungarian food and took us all on to the *Drei Husaren*, under the shadow of the now fully-restored Stephan Cathedral. It was a beautiful restaurant with green velvet armchairs and book-lined walls. Stefan was obviously a regular patron and the headwaiter fussed around him.

"And who is this beautiful young lady?"

"She is a wonderful Bulgarian dancer from the Opera."

"Bulgarian?" His eyes lit up and his chest pumped out with pride. "King Boris of Bulgaria dined here, I served him myself. We were Von Ribbentrop's favourite restaurant in all Vienna. He brought your King here the day he signed the Tripartite Pact with Hitler."

I looked at his smiling fawning face and my appetite disappeared. I saw them sitting there like ghosts, surrounded by the hated Nazi uniforms. There were times when you could not escape or forget the past. All I wanted was to go home. I got up and hurried out into Weihburggasse. Stefan followed behind me.

"What's wrong?"

"How could you, a Jew, eat in such a place?"

"I'm sorry, I did not know. Let's go somewhere else."

"No. I am going home."

"OK. Let me take you home." He hailed a passing taxi.

"No; I want to go home alone."

"May I see you tomorrow?"

"Stefan, you have so many girlfriends, why do you want me? Can't you see I'm difficult?"

"Dora, please let me see you." He had paid the driver before I realised it.

"Very well; but let me choose the restaurant."

After that he came almost nightly to the stage door, but always with a group of people. He was generous to everybody and spent his money with the sole intention of having a good time. Sometimes Gertie would come along but his attention was always fixed on me. Stefan was young, wealthy, Jewish and good-looking, what more could I want? He was not intellectual or artistically-minded and his manners were unpolished. Unlike Ferry, Carlos and my other admirers, he was awkward in showing his affection. He would bring me presents such as one would give a child – a monkey that would clap its hands when wound up, huge *papier-m*âché flowers, and a big white teddy bear that would keep my faithful doll company for the rest of their lives. It was as if I was a new specimen he had discovered and he was trying to find the way to win me. My lovers and admirers until now, had been much older than me; they had given me the education I had missed; I had trusted them and been enlightened by them. But I didn't trust Stefan – he was roughly the same age as Brazda, but Brazda had been so much more mature. Stefan was too young in himself to give me his undivided love. I wanted to be the only one – I didn't want to waste my energy on jealousy, or worrying where he was or how long our love would last. My heart had been broken twice already and I couldn't face having it broken again.

"Dora, I have been looking at the Opera programme. You are free this weekend," Stefan announced one day. "Will you go with me to Burgenland? I have a farmhouse there. I have a surprise waiting for you."

"Who else is coming?" I was curious to see what the surprise was but didn't want to put myself in a compromising situation.

He threw his arms up in the air. "Everyone!"

I wasn't impressed. 'Everyone' meant his two boring girlfriends and the other hangers-on.

"Bring clothes for riding. I want to show you some horses."

That sounded better. I missed riding in the Prater with Dudi, but I was still undecided.

"Kurtie is coming. He will pick you up on Saturday morning and you will be back on Sunday evening."

He had planned everything. I could hardly refuse if Kurtie was there. He would be the ideal chaperone.

"Very well, I'd love to."

Three cars arrived at our front door early on Saturday morning. Kurtie opened a door of the leading car, a Mercedes, and I sat next to him on the back seat. Stefan was driving with one of his well-endowed ladies, who hardly ever spoke, planted firmly beside him in the front. It was a long drive. Burgenland was a large province to the east of Vienna which formed most of the border with Hungary. It had been part of Hungary until after the First World War. The sun was shining and it was a beautiful autumnal day. We stopped for a snack of *wurst* and cheese and fresh wine before leaving the woody hills and entering a vast flat plain. I noticed big ditches overgrown with grass and asked Kurtie what they were.

"They were anti-tank ditches – part of the *Sudostwall* – the defence line the Nazis built with Jewish slave labour to keep out the Russians. It was a waste of time of course."

"What happened to the Jews?"

"Most were executed by the SS or died on death marches in the closing months of the war. They suffered terribly. Only the lucky ones survived."

Stefan was strangely quiet. I noticed the pain on his face in his driving mirror and wondered what he had gone through. I decided that I must be nicer to him.

We were heading east, the border, the Iron Curtain, with deadly mine fields and mile upon mile of barbed wire was only a few miles away. The entire aspect of the countryside was changing, as if we were travelling back into the past. We drove through little villages consisting of a few huts strewn along a single dirt road, which must have turned to thick mud in winter. We came at last to a village surrounded by vineyards and stopped at a two-storey building. Stefan began to organise everyone and everything in his usual flamboyant manner.

"I only have two bedrooms at my ranch. Kurtie, you will come with me, the rest of you will stay here at the hotel. Change into your riding clothes. I will be back in half an hour."

He turned to me. "Is that alright with you, Dora?"

"Yes, thank you, Stefan." I gave him a kiss on the cheek.

It was a typical country hotel, not luxurious, with comfortable settees and armchairs covered in flowery chintz. A vase of fresh flowers was on every table and bunches of dried flowers hung from the walls. Brightly-coloured peasant rugs were strewn over the scrubbed wooden floor. A smiling girl led the way upstairs to our rooms, off a sort of minstrel gallery that went around the lounge below. My room was like a doll's house, everything – bed head, cupboard, chairs and bedside table were painted with flowery patterns. There were even flowers on the sheets and eiderdown. I stepped out onto the small wooden balcony and looked into the distance. The ground was the colour of autumn leaves and the sky pale blue – a perfect afternoon for riding. I opened my suitcase and put on a pair of olive green ski pants and an olive green polo-necked jumper before pulling on a pair of olive green boots. I tied my hair in a ponytail and applied fresh mascara to my eyes before inspecting myself in the mirror inside the wardrobe. I was nearly nineteen but my figure was slender, more like a girl of fifteen. I still didn't wear a bra – there was hardly anything to hold up. I couldn't compare with the voluptuous girls that Stefan had brought along. Never mind – what I had was perfect for ballet.

I heard someone call my name and ran downstairs and outside into the dusty road, where Stefan, Kurtie and most of the others were waiting. Stefan took me by the hand and put me in his Mercedes.

"Kurtie, you bring the others. I want to show Dora the horses."

We sped out of the village and in the shortest of time came to a collection of buildings surrounded by a high wall. Stefan drove under a low arch into an enclosure that reminded me of the picture books of my childhood. Only these pictures were life-size. Horses of all colours and dimensions were looking out of the open tops of their stable doors. In the middle was a flat-roofed, pan-tiled house, with curtains neatly tied back at the windows and a whisk of sweet-smelling smoke coming out of the chimney.

I took a deep breath. "Stefan is this really yours?"

"Yes. Come and look at your surprise."

He led me towards a white horse that was looking at me with keen anticipation.

"Her name is Ambrosia. She's yours. She's your surprise."

I was stunned. "Stefan, I can't accept such a present."

He looked so disappointed; I couldn't help feeling sorry for him.

"Stefan, you must understand. I wouldn't know what to do with her. I couldn't afford to take care of her."

His face lit up. "She's yours and I will keep her here for you. You can ride her whenever you want; I will always arrange for you to be brought here."

I was overwhelmed. I stood there, stock still, with my arms hanging down beside me.

"Come on, try her out. Let's see if you like each other."

He handed me some sugar. I gave it her and stroked her head as the stable boy put on her saddle. Stefan helped me mount before he climbed on his own horse and we rode out under the arch on to the plain. Stefan looked even more magnificent on a horse and almost immediately broke into a canter. Ambrosia followed instantly. It was far different from the Prater with Dudi. There were no manicured rides bordered with chestnut trees; there was nothing in front of us at all, it felt as if we could go on riding forever. Stefan was an expert horseman – he was moulded to his horse. He instinctively knew the smoothest ways. I wondered if he had been born in this village. He drew up when we reached the top of a low hill; I just about managed to rein in Ambrosia beside him.

He smiled at me. I realised again how handsome he was. "We have ridden far enough. Let's turn back. Don't forget to bend your head as you go through the arch."

That night, Stefan announced he was taking us to his wine cellar for a tasting before dinner, and led us down the road to what looked like a little wooden hut. Once inside, we followed him down steep steps, cut out of the earth with wooden planks on top, which led deep into the ground. When we reached the bottom my eyes widened in disbelief – a cellar, dimly lit by candles, stretched into the darkness as far as I could see. Enormous wooden barrels were lined up left and right. The young girl, who had shown me to my room, was waiting with a tray of paper cones.

Stefan passed them around in his usual commanding

manner. "I would suggest you eat quite a lot during the tasting. I will help you later."

I looked at my cone. Inside were little brown squares. "What are they?"

"Dried pork fat. A local delicacy."

Dried pork fat? Salami was one thing for a Jewish girl, but dried pork fat was another. I put my cone back on the tray. The others ate and tasted heartily, as Stefan led us from barrel to barrel; I only tasted. It was a heavy red wine, I usually drank white, and I tasted far more than I intended. It became very hot in the cellar and I soon became desperate for fresh air. The others were too busy enjoying themselves to notice. I climbed back up the steps and opened the door of the hut. It hit me as soon as I stepped outside. I couldn't believe it – I flattened myself against the wall, thinking very hard.

'You mustn't make a fool of yourself in front of them. They are all still down below. Nobody can see you. The hotel is just down the road. All you have to do is to open the hotel door, walk through the lounge, go up the stairs, find your room and go to bed.'

I concentrated very hard. It was quite painful, but I was determined that I would walk as straight as a soldier. I made my way back along the street to the hotel. The passage across the lounge was the most difficult, but I was certain I had walked in a straight line. I stumbled a little on the stairs, but there it was my door – my room – my bed. I fell on to it – out to the world.

Next morning I woke with a heavy head and furry tongue to find myself beneath the sheet and eiderdown.

I was in my underwear. My clothes were all neatly folded on the chair. I was horrified. Who had taken off my clothes? Was it Stefan? What had he done to me? My frantic anxiety was interrupted by the smiling young maid with a steaming pot of coffee. Even the coffee pot was painted with flowers.

"Are you feeling better, Fraulein Reisser?"

"What happened to me?"

"Herr Watzig saw you leave the cellar and was very worried. He sent me to make sure you were all right. I saw you stagger through the lounge and was very surprised that you managed to get up the stairs. I knocked on your door but you were already fast asleep. I took off your boots, undressed you and put you to bed."

"How awful, I feel so ashamed. I won't be able to show my face."

"Don't worry, Fraulein Reisser. It happens all the time. The fresh air always does that when you come out of the cellar too quickly. Herr Watzig was very concerned. He hopes you feel better and is waiting for you downstairs."

I drank the coffee, had the hottest bath that I could bear and put on my riding gear again. I went downstairs with an olive green cape over my shoulders. I was still ashamed of myself – Papa would have been furious with me – I had certainly not behaved like a lady. Stefan was sitting alone, sipping his coffee, but looked up at me with great concern as I approached.

"Dora, are you alright? I've been so worried."

"I'm fine now, but I'm so sorry about last night."

"It was my fault. I should have warned you. Do you still feel like riding?"

"Yes. I think it will clear my head."

"Good. I've planned the entire day. The others have gone ahead. We will all ride to have lunch at a special spot I know. My carriage will take those who don't want to ride." He took my arm and led me out. "We will have a beautiful ride together, have a beautiful lunch and then have a beautiful ride back.

He drove me to the stables where Kurtie and the rest of the party were already mounted, with the exception of Stefan's two silent ladies, who were sitting in an open carriage looking their normal bored selves. I still felt shaky as Stefan helped me onto Ambrosia's back. Animals have unfailing instincts and she could feel my weakness. I had difficulty controlling her and we had only gone half a mile of so when, without any warning, she reared up on her hind legs, turned and galloped back towards the stables. I clung on for dear life, hearing Stefan's anxious shouts of "Dora! Dora!" behind me. I only just remembered to duck my head as we raced under the arch. Ambrosia calmed down immediately she entered the enclosure. I patted her neck and told her sternly never to do it again.

"Are you sure you want to ride? You can easily go in the carriage with the other girls." Stefan had caught up with and was full of concern.

I shook my head. I was determined never to be just one of the other girls. I turned Ambrosia round and cantered gently out to join the other riders. We rode for nearly an hour across the smooth plain, with the carriage following behind us, until a house appeared out of the middle of nowhere. Stefan stood up in his stirrups and pointed towards it.

"Gallop to the house. Lunch is waiting!"

He set off at an alarming speed, the others following cautiously behind. I followed even more cautiously, with Stefan's ladies and their bosoms bouncing about behind me in their carriage. It must have been quite a sight.

A short, sturdy man, dressed in a voluminous shirt with trousers tucked in his boots, was standing at the door of the house.

"Tafika!"

Stefan dismounted and embraced him as they laughed and joked in Hungarian. Tafika then invited us inside where a huge wood fire was crackling in the fireplace, and a long wooden table with gleaming glasses of schnapps and benches with welcoming soft cushions awaited us. A gramophone was playing Hungarian music as we toasted each other with schnapps. Tafika's wife, a big, friendly peasant woman, served us hot goulash soup, followed by a roasted piglet with boiled potatoes and plums. Her husband filled our glasses with dark red Tokai wine.

I was still feeling the effects of the previous night. "Stefan, I won't be able to ride Ambrosia back."

"Don't worry. Tafika will bring us back in his carriage."

I relaxed and allowed myself another glass of Tokai. *Tschardasch*, a traditional folk dance, began to play on the gramophone. I jumped on the long table and began to dance, faster and faster with the pace of the music; others joined me and we sang and danced in joyous, carefree abandon until the autumn sun began to sink through the window. It was time to journey back from this enchantment. It had become cold outside. I wrapped my cloak about me and Stefan put a blanket over our knees as he sat next to me in Tafika's two-seated carriage. Tafika's long whip cracked and we were off with the cold air rushing towards us, pushing us back into our seat. I found myself snuggling against Stefan's comforting warmth. He took my hand and put a little box in it. I looked at him questioningly.

"Open it."

It was a diamond ring.

"We are now engaged."

The enchantment of the day was vanishing as swiftly as Cinderella's finery at the prince's ball.

"Stefan, I don't want to be engaged."

"Then marry me straight away."

Marry? And give up my dancing? My contract with Cranko in Stuttgart was only a few months away. Marry? And give up my freedom? To be like all the other Jewish girls, security, children, no excitement, no anticipation of the unexpected? Besides, I didn't love him. My heart still yearned for Brazda. If I could have loved Stefan, I would have gladly taken his ring, his horse and all the other wonderful things he wanted to lavish on me without the slightest hesitation. But I knew I would never be able to fulfil his expectations.

I put the ring back in his hand. "Stefan, I can't."

He looked so hurt. I had ruined the perfect day that he had so carefully planned.

I put my hand on his. "Please be my friend," I asked.

He stared out across the endless plain and didn't say another word.

19

Heartbreak

It was middle of December and we were in full rehearsal for a new ballet with the Vienna Philharmonic. There was little time left. The performance went out live on Eurovision on New Year's Day. In the evening we had a performance of *Kiss Me Kate*. Towards the end of my dance, I climbed on top of the pile of packing cases, as I had done so many times before. The stage was in semi-darkness, but I felt the warmth of the spotlight upon me. I danced passionately, feeling the familiar music pulsating through my body as it built to a crescendo; I jumped on cue, turned perfectly, expecting to fall into safe hands, but that night there was nobody to catch me and I crashed down to the stage on my back. Some idiot had missed a cue and the others had simply followed like sheep. They stood around me paralysed, but I got up quickly and finished my dance. I screamed my head off at them in the wings before I went furiously to my dressing room.

Fred Leever, who had been watching as normal from the wings, rushed in. "Dora, are you alright? I never thought you would be able to get up."

I was still raging. "They are so stupid; they don't use their brains. On top of that they are not even good dancers."

He took me in his arms and cuddled me. "Calm down. We'll have dinner after the show."

We had dinner. I always appreciated his friendship and sympathy.

I worked as usual the next day and the day after, but I began to feel a pain in the front of my body near my lungs. By the end of the week the pain was excruciating; breathing was difficult, I had moments of panic and I was sure I had pneumonia. I decided to see Dr Sponberger; I had always liked and trusted him.

"I am sure there is nothing serious," I said confidently.

He smiled but after examining me, announced, "Dora, it is not your lungs."

"But it hurts where my lungs are."

"Does your back hurt as well?"

"Yes, but in ballet you are always pulling some muscle or another. It will go away."

"Anything else?"

"My breathing bothers me and I have difficulty moving my right hand."

He took me for an X-ray. While we waited for the result we chatted about our families – Christel, his daughter, my friend from boarding school, was studying to become a doctor like her father. I was proud of her and wished her well. I remembered her love of books. She has the brain for it, I thought.

The nurse came back with the X-ray. He put it up to the light. Why was he becoming so quiet?

"Dora, it's your vertebrae not your lungs."

"It can't be." I sat on the examining bed.

He sat beside me and continued talking, calmly and reassuringly, but his words just passed by me. Vertebrae, back – I knew what it meant.

"Are you dancing?"

"Of course, every night; and rehearsing for the New Year's Day ballet."

"You must stop."

"I can't. I have a contract for the Stuttgart Ballet."

"Dora, you have injured your back very seriously. If you don't stop now and we don't correct it, you will never be able to dance again."

"And if I stop will I get completely better?"

"We will get a second opinion of course, but I'm afraid there will be some things which you will never be able to do."

"The Eurovision performance is only in a few days. I have a very important part in it, I can't let them down and I won't – can you get me through it?"

I could see the pity in his eyes. He had known me since I was a child. "Yes, I suppose so, with painkiller injections."

"Thank you. I will keep the rehearsals short. Please be with me on the day."

"I will, Dora."

I jumped off the bed and went out into the street. Anger was piling up within me. Not to be able to do everything? For a dancer that was impossible. If anybody thinks I will give in, they don't know me. I didn't take a tram. I walked for hours; even that was painful. I eventually sat down on a bench on the

Ring near the Rathaus. The anger had gone. I didn't feel anything anymore – no anger, no sadness. Only emptiness. The ornate buildings and architecture around me no longer had any interest. I was an island all to myself.

Perhaps Dr Sponberger is wrong, perhaps the second opinion will say that I will be perfect again. With that hope, I went home.

Mama sensed something was wrong, but I couldn't tell her. If I talked about it I would almost be confirming it to myself.

In the evening, the telephone rang outside in the hall. The landlady answered.

"Dora, it's for you."

It was Doctor Sponberger. "I'm so sorry, I was right. My colleague has seen your X-ray and agrees with my diagnosis. I want to see you again. I will come to the Volksoper if it's easier for you."

"Very well. Thank you. Tomorrow at two."

Mama listened but didn't say anything. She knew she would hear it all in the end. There was no cosy, loving chat that night; we ate our supper in silence. I pretended to be tired and went to bed early. Breathing hurt me, my back was in agony and my right hand was in pain. I took one of the pills that Dr Sponberger had given me and eventually fell asleep.

"Madame Luca, may I have a word with you?"

"Of course, Dora."

I knew I was her favourite dancer. Her little prima

196

ballerina. Her efforts and belief in me had taken me to the top. Say it quickly Dora I thought.

"I've seen a doctor. I have injured my back and won't be able to dance anymore. I will finish after the New Year ballet."

"Dora, it must be a mistake."

I looked at her and fell into her arms crying. She cried with me.

"Dora, tell me everything."

I told her what I remembered of what Doctor Sponberger had said.

"Dora, I will create a new ballet especially for you. You will hardly have to do any dancing it will be more acting than dancing – you have such personality." She was stroking my hair, fumbling for words, trying to reassure the both of us.

"And what after that, Madame Luca? Watching the younger dancers overtaking me? Seeing them taking over my parts and not being able to fight it?"

She didn't reply. She understood. It would have broken me even more.

"Please don't change anything until the New Year – I will leave after that."

I didn't rehearse, didn't train and the few performances I had left were not demanding. Even so, Madame Luca changed and rearranged things so I had practically nothing to do. She stood next to me every night before I stepped on stage. Dr Sponberger was also there, leaning on his crutches. I hadn't asked him to, but he was there, and took me home afterwards. I knew my parts, the parts I had worked and fought for, had been distributed to others and the company were rehearsing vigorously throughout the day. The show had to go on. I had nothing to do now but wait for my last performance. Every movement was painful, as if a tight iron clasp was around my back and chest. I lay in bed and Mama sat beside me. My right hand lay on the bed – it was getting more difficult for me to move it. My left hand was in Mama's. We stayed like that for hours. I still couldn't believe it. But I had something to hold on to – the Eurovision ballet.

Dr Sponberger came to pick me up early in the morning of New Year's Day.

I kissed Mama goodbye. "Mama, wait and see; I will be brilliant."

She held me close to her breast and all her love poured out of her. Dr Sponberger helped me into his car and we drove off.

When we arrived at the hall where the transmission would take place, nobody mentioned my back. That was what I wanted. A dresser helped me into my costume and I carefully tied the ribbons of my ballet shoes for the last time. The television cameras and lights were all in place; everybody was quiet and tense, waiting for the cue. Dr Sponberger gave me my injection and the ballet began. I couldn't feel any pain at all; it was as if nothing was wrong with me. I forgot my injuries and let myself go completely, until suddenly there was a stabbing pain in my back. I froze. Gerhardt, my partner, dragged me behind the camera, where Dr Sponberger gave me another injection. I continued with the dance, more carefully, but I began to feel dizzy. I kept going but fainted as the dance ended.

I regained consciousness in hospital. Mama was at my bedside. And then I cried. I cried like I'd never cried before. It wasn't crying, it was screaming.

"No! No, no, not me! Why Mama why? Please God, don't take that away from me. It's my life. It can't stop. I'm only eighteen." I prayed and screamed and cried with pain everywhere. But I didn't want to die, whatever that might be; I wanted to live. I was given another injection and fell asleep.

I woke with a dry mouth. Mama was still next to me and gave me something to drink. I felt as if all my boundless energy had been drained from my body. I couldn't move my right hand and my neck was so stiff. I just lay there, waiting – wondering what would come next. Dr Sponberger came into the room. He put a hand tenderly on Mama's shoulder. Poor Mama, she looked up at him, imploring him for good news.

He sat on my bed. "Dora, we are going to make you better. You must have patience."

It was the one thing I wasn't blessed with. He smiled, knowing me only too well.

"We will put a plaster on your body and a metal structure at your back to hold your neck. You can take it off for comfort when you go to bed, but otherwise I want you to wear it all the time." The usual 'Why? was about to form on my lips but he was too quick. "Dora, please don't fight with me, you know I want you to get better.

There was no point in arguing. They wheeled me into another room and put the plaster on my body and fitted the contraption for my neck. The smell of the plaster nauseated me. Standing there naked, being held by two nurses, made me feel helpless. They tried to make jokes.

"You look like a beautiful statue."

"You'll soon get used to it. It will only be for a few months."

Months? How many months? I stood there, not saying a word.

Although I could walk, they put me into a wheelchair and Mama took me to a taxi. The wheelchair was supposed to be only for the first few days until I got used to the extra weight on my body. The nurses wanted me to take it home with me, but I refused to let them put it in the taxi. I was determined never to sit in it again. The drive home was short. Thank God the apartment was on the ground floor. I was exhausted.

I lay in bed silently for days. Mama fed me and waited with her incredible patience for me to speak. Papa stayed in the other room and looked in from time to time. I couldn't smile as I usually did when I saw him. He understood. After those terrible months in the punishment camp, nobody understood pain better than him. I knew I was so lucky to have such parents. I watched them sitting anxiously together in my room and knew they were completely united again, like they were in my memories in Bulgaria before the war. The pills I took made me sleep a great deal, but when I woke one of my parents was always there, and I slowly began to accept the inevitable. One morning, when Papa was beside me, I opened the drawer by my bed, took the precious contract for Stuttgart that Swartz, the agent, had so meticulously negotiated for me, crumpled it up and let it fall to the floor. It was final. I would never dance again.

"Papa, please could you write to the Volksoper and tell them I have resigned."

Their letter of acknowledgement came back almost immediately, as if they were relieved to let me go. My career had been ended by their incompetence but I had no thought or knowledge of compensation, it was virtually unknown in those days. The Volksoper was run by the Austrian state; if I had wanted to pursue it, I would have received a pension for life – but I would probably have been too proud to accept it.

I had no idea how many weeks or months passed. Until one day I saw that the sky was blue.

"Mama, let's go for a walk." I began to fit on my neck piece. "We'll have to camouflage this contraption and figure out what I can wear so I don't look like a monster." We went into a long conversation over my wardrobe, which made me forget my troubles for a while.

We went for walks every day after that. Walks and then back to bed. The pain was still there and my right arm was still stiff. Papa would come with my favourite patisseries or sometimes a bottle of champagne.

"Papa, if I continue eating and drinking like this, the plaster will burst."

We laughed then but I still cried alone at night, biting into my little pillow.

I realised one day that nobody from the ballet had come to see me or tried to make contact with me. Either they didn't know, or if they knew they didn't know how to react, or perhaps Mama had not let them see me. I didn't bother me. They wouldn't make me better.

Two months passed. It was the end of February, my nineteenth birthday. Hardy phoned from Germany, Papa gave me flowers and Mama made a cake. Nineteen years old and what was going to happen to me?

"Mama, I'm going to the Volksoper to say hello."

I took a taxi to the stage door and walked in. The doorkeeper looked up at me from his newspaper. I nodded at him.

"Where do you think you're going?"

He couldn't mean me. I continued walking towards the stairs as I had done so many, many times.

"Hey, you there, what do you think you're doing?"

I looked round. There was nobody else. He was new. I'd never seen him before.

"I'm Dora Reisser."

"Who?"

"Dora Reisser," I said loudly.

"So what?"

I wanted to say – 'Listen, you idiot. I have been here for years. I was the best dancer in the ballet,' – but I didn't say a word. I just looked at him in disbelief. After only two months my name is forgotten, as if I never existed? But why should I expect anything different? People gaze at blazing stars in wonder, but ignore them and seek others as soon as they burn out. Sitting and crying over spilt milk was a waste of time. I swept out past him. It was time to move on.

"Mama, I'm leaving Vienna."

I had had enough of this city and its bitter-sweet people. I had never trusted them completely and there was nothing to hold me here. My parents were ready to leave too: they had only really stayed because of me. As Mama helped me pack my belongings, I came across the shoebox containing Ferry's presents and letters. I looked at the little drawings he had made especially for me. Even after Brazda, I could still feel the pain. I put them back, together with all the other gifts from Carlos and Dudi and closed the box.

"Mama, I am leaving these with you."

20

Munich and Geneva

Hardy was now making good money in Germany and I decided to join him there. He was the most generous of brothers. He rented me a small one-room studio apartment in Munich and bought me a second-hand Opel to get around in. Germany was in the full flow of its economic miracle, and Munich, bang in the centre of the American zone, was flourishing rapidly. It had far fewer ruins than Vienna. The people were friendly and more down to earth, busy working their way to success. I went to a hairdresser and cut my long hair to shoulder length and had a soft perm – the ballerina look had gone; new hair for a new life. I now had plenty of time to read and wanted to expand my mind. I read Jean-Paul Sartre, Albert Camus and David Roussett, but couldn't agree with their communist sentiments and philosophy. They ignored the injustice and lack of freedom that people were forced to accept in the Soviet Bloc. I had witnessed it in Bulgaria and only too recently with Brazda. I admired Tito who had stood up to the mighty Soviet Union and survived. The avant-garde films I saw, focussed on past injustices, insanity, torture and crime, left me in despair. I wanted to look forward with optimism to the future.

Most of Hardy's Jewish friends from Vienna had

now moved to Munich. It was a more open society; less anti-Semitic and easier to prosper in. Hardy also had new friends, some of whom were German. They were always eager to explain to me that they were too young to have had anything to do with the Nazi regime and how their parents had suffered under it; there was a new Germany now and Nazism had been eradicated forever. I counted back the years and knew that they were not too young to have been members of the Hitler Youth, and couldn't understand that if so many had been against the Nazis, how had the Nazis ever got into power? But I said nothing. I went to parties and dinners at their homes, boating on the lakes, country picnics and beerhalls, although my desire for a new joyful life was often in conflict with my conscience.

I was not short of admirers – there was an architect, a businessman and a restauranteur. I wanted to avoid any thought of dancing and ballet, but the plaster was a constant reminder. I had to scratch myself with a long thin stick when it itched. I couldn't even take a bath but had to wash myself with a sponge. I finally had enough.

"Hardy, I want my plaster off."

"Dora, it's too early."

"I don't care; I'm going to the hospital tomorrow and having it taken off."

It came off. My skin was shrivelled up but now I could scratch it to my heart's content. I felt as light as a bird, free of chains.

Fraulein Reisser, you mustn't run, take it very easy. We will make you a special corset but it will take some time."

I didn't listen. I was jubilant. I could move my head, my arm. I felt perfect again. I understood ballet was out of the question, but I wasn't going to accept restrictions on anything else

"Hardy, let's give a party."

We invited all our Jewish friends. On the day of the party the telephone rang.

"Hi, Dora, it's Hubert Dilworth, from Vienna, remember me?. How are you? I'm in town; your mother gave me your number."

"Hubert, you've come on just the right day – I'm having a party tonight at seven. You must come."

Hubert, my dear gentle friend – I was looking so much to seeing him.

Hardy loved shopping and went to the market and bought the best cheese and salami and all sorts of bread and plenty of beer and wine. He stood at the door greeting the guests, while I sat on the sofa, trying to be a perfect hostess, feeling quite exuberant. There was laughter and happy conversation until Hubert walked in. The room was suddenly silent as I got up and embraced him warmly. I gave him a kiss and asked him to sit next to me. I couldn't believe it, but some of the guests began to leave.

Bummi, one of Hardy's oldest friends from Vienna, came over, "Dora, can I have a word?"

I got up, with some difficulty, and followed him to the other side of the room.

"How can you invite him here with us?"

"What do you mean?"

"He doesn't fit in with us. You should have warned us before he came."

"How can you say that?"

"It's him or us."

"Because he's black?"

My blood was at boiling point. After all the persecution and prejudice we Jews had gone through, how could they behave like this?

"He stays and the rest of you can go."

The room began to empty fast. Hubert understood what was happening.

"Don't worry, Dora. I'll leave."

"Hubert, you are a mensch."

"I've been called lots of things. What is a mensch?"

"A good human being. We are going out to dinner, just the two of us. Don't let me down. You are my date."

Hardy rented a flat for our parents in Schwabing, the bohemian quarter of Munich, I left the studio to join them and we were happily reunited. Mama and I had so much to tell each other that Papa hardly got a word in. We soon settled into a routine, Papa would grind the beans and make coffee for breakfast, Mama would sew and keep the house in order and look after me and we would have our chats again at bedtime. I had been fitted for the corset, when it finally arrived I put it on and looked at myself in the mirror. It was pink, like an old lady's corset, except that it had a metal support at the back. I sent it back immediately and stipulated that it had to be in black and inlaid with lace and look sexy. They did the best they could and I wore it and tried to forget it, but the pain was always there, especially in the mornings. I made every effort to be happy and content, but Mama could see how restless I was.

"Dorale, you should think about getting married. You'll make a good wife. There are many well-to-do Jewish men that would be happy to have you. You are charming; know how to entertain… You would be an asset to any of them."

"There isn't anyone I want."

"Issac is a lovely man so is Ivan. They like you, I can tell."

"Mama, please stop it. I don't want to get married."

I still had no idea what I would do with my life, but I had no desire to spend the rest of it married in Munich.

"Benno is doing better than ever in Geneva – Hardy is thinking of working for him. Why don't you go and visit him again?"

I was once again on a plane to Geneva, but this time without Ron. As I expected, Benno was not at the airport to meet me, but a handsome, well-dressed man was waiting with my name on a small board.

"Dora Reisser?"

I nodded.

"Great. Bernie's been delayed and asked me to pick you up and take you to the hotel."

Hotel? At least I was not in the little room on the ground floor – I had had more than my fill of little rooms.

"And who are you?"

"Richard Hammerman, call me Dick. I'm a director of IOS."

"It's very kind of you."

"No problem. I'm staying there myself."

He was a cultured American, entertaining with a charming smile. As we drove to the hotel I learned more about Investors Overseas Services. Bernie believed it was no longer enough to invest in a fund that invested in all the top companies, Bernie proposed to invest directly in all the top funds. He was starting his own fund – The Fund of Funds – and Dick Hammerman was going to manage it. I was fascinated how one could make so much money without actually working for it. I knew nothing about business or stocks and shares; I had never even possessed a cheque book, and when we arrived at the hotel Dick paid for my room with a credit card – I had never seen or heard of such a thing before.

Bernie arrived later on a private plane and Dick took me back to the airport to meet him. When he sauntered through the doors, I was glad to see that Françoise was not with him, but he had replaced her with three others, who were trailing dutifully behind. He had put on weight, his face had become round. He seemed pleased to see me.

"Hello, my little cousin."

Thank God he didn't call me ballerina any more. Bernie and Dick talked business non-stop as we drove back to Geneva. My back was hurting as I sat crammed in the back with the three girls. Bernie's offices had expanded like him – they now occupied three floors in Rue de Lausanne. He told me in the lift that he would soon be taking over the entire building. He swept into his office where his top men were waiting anxiously for him, eager to carry out his orders, blind devotion shining from their eyes. It made me think of Napoleon and his Marshals. I sat on the periphery with the three girls and waited for Bernie, like everyone else.

It was the same over the next few days. Bernie went everywhere with a group, who seemed to spend most of their time waiting for Bernie. I soon became bored with it and spent more time on my own.

"Dora, the Vienna Ballet is in Geneva," Bernie announced laconically one morning. "Do you want to see them?"

"Yes, I suppose so." Would I be able to sit and watch them dancing?

"Good. I'll get my secretary to arrange a ticket for you."

I wasn't sure I would be strong enough. "Benno, will you come with me?"

He shrugged. "OK."

"Bernie, it's important for me not to be alone."

"I'll be there, and why don't you invite your friends to come to my apartment afterwards? We can order some food from Movenpick."

"That would be great."

I spent the day ordering the food and went to the

apartment to see it was delivered before the show. Delicate canapés of smoked salmon, caviar, cheese and salami were artistically arranged on silver platters. Sweet shells of pastry were filled with an assortment of fruits in jelly, topped with cream. Another platter was overflowing with *petit fours*. I had bought two big vases of roses. It all looked magnificent, laid out on the long table. Wine and champagne were stacked in Bernie's great American fridge. Everything was ready – apart from Bernie. I had arranged to meet him there so we could go together. I looked at my watch and decided to phone him. It was getting late.

"Dora, I've no time to go there and pick you up. Take a taxi; I'll meet you at the theatre."

I arrived at the theatre. People streamed in past me but there was no sign of Bernie. I stood there alone in my rust-gold duchesse silk satin cocktail dress. I opened my little bag and took out the two tickets; small, square, purple-coloured pieces of paper. The overture began. I had to go in. I went over to the ticket office, moving very slowly. I was unsure of myself, I wasn't wearing my corset.

"If Mr Cornfeld comes, please give him this."

Bernie had got the best seats, right in the middle of the front row. I sat down stiffly as the curtain opened. I scanned the faces of the dancers – it was not the full company – where were Gertie and Lisle? – At least they would understand. I watched my dances being danced by somebody else. It was almost as if I was watching my lover making love to somebody new. The interval came. I didn't move. The audience streamed out, chatting happily and came chatting happily back. Bernie was not among them. The lights went out again and my assurance drained out of me. I was in despair. Silent tears rolled down my cheeks. My hand was still clutching my little purple ticket. I put it in my bag and promised myself that I would keep it forever to remind me of this terrible night. It ended at last. Applause burst out all round – as it once did for me. Bunches of flowers were presented, the lights came back on and the audience went happily home. I was the last one in the theatre, sitting alone on my red velvet chair. I carefully got up. I was about to face my nightmare alone. I walked up the stairs to the dressing rooms. I knocked and went in, my ex-colleagues looked at me, confused and perplexed, as if I were an unwelcome guest at a wedding.

"You were all great."

"Dora! What are you doing here?"

"I've come to invite you all to a wonderful party."

I was grateful they didn't ask how I was. I behaved as if nothing had changed.

About a dozen jumped into some taxis at the stage door and we drove off to Bernie's apartment. I was chatting away merrily, working my optimism overtime. I opened the door and led them in. Bernie's cats had had a banquet. They lay sleeping stretched out on the floor. The beautifully arranged silver trays were in chaos. Food was scattered all over the floor. It was the final straw. I started to cry.

"Dora, there's no reason to cry, it's funny." someone said. "They haven't drunk the drinks have they?"

I couldn't stop.

"Dora, please, it's not important."

They opened the champagne and raided Bernie's fridge for food. I couldn't wait for them to leave. When they had finally gone, I lay on the floor and closed my eyes. Where am I going? What am I going to do? All my energy had been absorbed by ballet, I need to turn it onto another track, or otherwise I would burn out. Always the same quandary – the same questions – they never left me. I knew that I would have to answer them by myself.

21

Israel 1958

I had always wanted to visit Israel and decided that this was the time. The sensation of stepping off the plane was one of the most emotional experiences of my life. As I walked the few steps to the so-called airport building to pick up my suitcase, the smell of jasmine was floating in the air. I breathed in deeply – hardly believing that I had made it at last. A porter came to help me with my suitcase. I wanted to tell him not to carry it – we are all equal here, but didn't want to strain my back and gave him a big tip. I showed my Austrian passport, of which I had been so proud when Papa had bought in Vienna in those early days after the war. The pretty girl smiled and said 'Shalom' as she stamped it, and I wanted to kiss her. I followed the other passengers out of the small building. People were crying, embracing, deliriously happy at seeing friends and relatives again. Uncle Salomon and Aunt Fanny were among them, smiling at me. After many hugs and kisses, they guided me carefully to their car, very conscious of my corset.

It was early evening. All I could see, far into the distance, was bare land. No houses. The road we were driving on wasn't doing Uncle Salomon's car any good either. The sea soon appeared and I could see low buildings with big drums perched on the top.

"What are those barrels on the roof?"

"Our hot water tanks; the sun supplies the heat."

The sun was going down but it was still very hot. I was sweating beneath my corset. My aunt and uncle were living in a newly-built apartment house in Tel Aviv, close to the concert hall.

"It was still desert here when we came," said Aunt Fanny proudly. "It's a most desirable area now."

Uncle Salomon's plumbing skills, which had been looked down on when he had first entered the family, had proved invaluable in the rapid building of the city and by Israeli standards he was comparatively well-off. Neither of them had changed, we continued as when we had last seen each other in Sofia. Uncle Salomon was as protective towards me as he had always been, and Aunt Fanny began at once feeding me with all my favourite Bulgarian delicacies that had been unavailable in Vienna: smoked lacerda fish, sirena and kashkaval cheese, and baklava dripping with honey. Aunt Fanny didn't stop talking. Lilli, despite losing her leg, was very happy studying medicine in France, and Nina was already married and was living with her husband and child in a kibbutz, near the Lebanese border.

Nina was waiting in the middle of the compound when Uncle Salomon drove me to visit her. She had always been the youngest and most delicate of the three of us, but here she stood, her hair bleached from the sun, her face tanned from working in the fields, still the same height as me, but her physique so much stronger and tougher. It was the same with so many. These were not the pale-faced, round-shouldered Jews of Europe, but a new and vibrant race, proud and devoted to defending their precious little land. There were barely two million of them then, the country was so small, you could cross it half an hour in some places, they were surrounded by five hostile neighbours, heavily armed by Russia, but I knew that they would never let it go.

Nina introduced me to her husband, Yoel, a tall, strong, blonde young man with piecing blue eyes, and then gave us tea in the dining room – a flattish building, furnished with the barest of necessities.

"We eat lots of fruit and vegetables, morning, lunch and evening. The chicken farm supplies the rest." Everything she said was matter of fact, short and to the point.

Nina's little son was with the other children in another building, away from their mothers and fathers, where they slept, learnt and played. Special hours were put aside for them to be with their parents. I was very surprised at this, knowing my own Jewish mother and our way of life and upbringing. Not being close to your parents seemed very strange to me.

"We have to work," Nina explained, "men and women – all the same."

The little beds were made up tidily, the toys neatly put away, the low tables piled with books. In the corridor, leading to the bathroom area, there were shelves with name tags on which were laid out towels, soap and toothbrushes in perfect order. She led us outside to the playground, to the sounds of singing, laughter and childish prattle. The children were all dressed in the same shorts and shirts and little hats, for protection against the merciless sun. Nina pointed out her little boy, Elan, who was playing happily, and smiled as if to say, 'You see; it works.' We walked through grass and the shade of newly planted trees to Nina's living quarters – a small wooden house, almost a hut. Inside there were only three beds, three chairs and a table, but on the shelves were books and books and books.

"In the evenings, we are all studying something or the other," Nina casually explained. "My subject is psychiatry."

Early rising, working in the fields, sharing everything together. A weekly meeting where decisions affecting their lives were taken cooperatively. Yet they each had their own individual identities and opinions. Was this the real socialism?

I remembered my days camping with the Gordonia. "Nina, do you have to stand guard at night?"

"Yes."

"If you see someone approaching the compound, what would you do?"

"Shoot."

I was full of admiration, but I somehow felt that life on a kibbutz was not for me.

The following day I was taken to see the rest of the family, who were living in Jaffa, along with most of the other 40,000 Bulgarian immigrants. First call was on Aunt Eleanora, who now lived alone. My kindly tutor,

Uncle Hertz, who spoke twelve languages but couldn't earn a penny, had died soon after arriving. Eleanora was as ferocious as ever. We were not allowed to walk on the white tiles in the hall, only on the black. My two aunts embarked immediately on their continuous complaint about the heat. Air conditioning was a distant dream even in America; in Israel you were lucky if you had a small electric fan. We then went on to Grandmother Rachel was also living alone. Her poor son, my uncle, Danny, who had been forbidden to marry his Christian sweetheart, had become more and more disturbed and was now in a mental institution. No one could say whether this was due to his broken heart or his experiences during the war.

Grandmother Rachel, whose exact age had always been a mystery, was feeling unwell and was in bed smoking a Turkish cigarillo when we arrived. She nevertheless wasted little time in ordering everybody around.

"Eleanora, bring out the cups and sugar and jam. Fanny, warm the samovar and pour the tea."

"Grandmother, how old are you?" I asked as she gave me a smoky kiss.

"Seventy-two," she replied amid much coughing and croaking.

"Mother, how can you say you are only seventy-two when your oldest daughter Sophie is sixty?" protested Eleanora.

There was even more coughing and croaking. "You are lying on my deathbed."

Knowing smiles spread all round the room.

Tel Aviv was a fun city even then. The busy cafes along the main street, Dizengoff, were like a never-ending street party. You couldn't be bored. Everyone was interested in everything. Everybody had their own point of view and was determined to prove their point. Golda Meir said Israel was a country with two million prime ministers. And it was impossible to be lonely. Everyone seemed to know everybody and everybody seemed to know somebody. Many were in army uniform, men and women, blonde and blue-eyed or dark and olive-skinned, beautiful creatures, a wonderful mixture of races and cultures, Russian, Polish, Bulgarian, Moroccan, Yemeni, and so many, many others. Looking at them helped me forget my pain. But on Friday afternoon the town came to a standstill, the streets were deserted. The religious minority had made sure that strict rules were enforced – much to Aunt Fanny's annoyance.

"They will not even let you watch football."

"But Aunt Fanny, you don't like football and you never watched football."

"It doesn't matter, if I like or not like; if I want, I want."

I talked with everyone and soon acquired some new friends. One of them, Ruti, a vibrant, raven-haired young architect, invited me to a chamber concert at the newly built Dan hotel.

"Music has always been vitally important here," she explained as we walked along the beach, past the uninspired structure of the Sheraton, the only other big hotel in Tel Aviv at that time. "Huberman founded the

Israeli Philharmonic Orchestra in 1936. So many of the finest musicians in Germany and Austria were Jewish, the Nazis wouldn't let them work there so they came here. Thank God they did. You have to imagine how it was then. There were hardly any roads – they had to carry their heavy instruments through the sand, bumping into camels. Most of them are still alive. Some will be playing tonight."

We entered the tall modern hotel and were shown into a medium sized hall. Most of the seats were already taken and Ruti began greeting and chatting; she knew everybody. We sat down as the lights dimmed. A man in front of me turned and smiled. He had receding hair and twinkling black eyes, casually almost scruffily dressed like most Israeli men.

"Hallo, Ruti," he said in a rich deep voice, "who is your beautiful friend?"

"Shalom Dan, this is Dora."

The girl seated next to him turned and nodded.

"Shalom."

She was very attractive, with wild long black hair framing an olive–coloured face. Her eyes were big, radiant and smouldering.

The music began. He turned again and fixed his eyes upon me. I couldn't listen to the music. He could have picked me up, turned me round in mid-air and put me down again. I wouldn't have resisted.

The interval came and he and the girl followed us into the lobby. I could feel that his eyes were still on me, but tried to appear completely unconcerned.

"Who is Dan, Ruti?"

"One of the finest architects in Israel; he is designing the new Museum of Art."

"Who is the beauty?"

"His latest girlfriend; she says she is a poet."

As we went back to our seats, he quickly asked where I was staying in Tel Aviv, what was I doing and how long I intended staying in Israel.

I was only able to answer his first question.

The following morning, Uncle Solomon was listening to his fourth news broadcast of the day.

"He listens in German, Russian, and Spanish and Hebrew," Aunt Fanny explained, "it's exactly the same news."

"Then why does he listen?"

"There are always different nuances," Uncle Solomon growled.

The doorbell rang. It was Dan.

"What are you doing here?"

"I was passing on my way to work. Will you have coffee with me?"

He was a typical Israeli, straight to the point.

We went to a nearby coffee house.

"You didn't answer my question last night. How long are you staying here?"

"I'm not sure. I've never been to Israel before and I love it. I want to see more of it."

"Great, I'll show it you."

"Which country do you come from?"

"Israel. I was born here in a kibbutz."

"How did you become an architect?"

"I wanted to build my country; and I am brilliant."

We both laughed.

He came the following evening, dressed in his usual messy way, and took me to his car, which looked as if it hadn't been washed since he had bought it – on the other hand, I suppose water was very scarce. The car was full of plans, blueprints and books. He made a place for me to sit and we drove along the coast. Small boats, very much the worse for wear, were scattered all along the beach.

"What are they?"

"They ferried refugees in at night from Cyprus and from the big ships that the British did not allow to come in. I belonged to the Haganah. Our job was to get them off the beach as quickly as possible. They staggered in and we would shout 'Run! Run! Run!' We had to get them into the town where they could hide, before the British saw them. One night, they waded on to the beach and the English soldiers were there waiting. We ran towards the refugees to protect them. Some were so weak and exhausted they could hardly stand. A British officer screamed through a loud-hailer, 'Everyone in wet clothes stay where they are. Don't move. The rest of you come back here.' We simply took our dry clothes off, gave them to the refugees and put on their wet ones. The British just stared at us. After a while they lowered their guns and left, and more Jews got into Israel."

I warmed to him even more and squeezed his hand.

We drove a little further to the old Ottoman quarter of Jaffa, which was clinging around a hill overlooking the harbour.

"We are going to an Arab restaurant."

"Is it safe?"

"Of course, I live here."

He took me into a stone building right on the harbour quay, very simple, with benches and plain wooden tables. Arabs in European and traditional clothes were sitting alongside casually dressed Israelis. Everybody knew Dan; he had obviously been there many times. The waiters were friendly and the food was delicious.

"I didn't know that Jews and Arabs lived so close together."

"Why not? We have so much in common if the politicians would leave us alone. I have been in two wars already and I don't want to be in anymore. We must build this country, the entire Middle East, together."

He told me passionately of his plans, the buildings and projects he had teeming around in his mind: art galleries, theatres, housing projects. Ferry had taught me to love architecture and it was inspiring to listen to Dan's dreams. He wanted to build roads across the deserts, bringing countries closer together, exchanging knowledge, help and trade. The moon was sparkling on the water as we came out of the restaurant. The fishing boats looked so romantic in the harbour. Dan sensed my mood and bent down and kissed me. It was time for me to love again. I let him take my hand and lead me to his old stone house on top of the hill.

Over the next few weeks, whenever he was free, he showed me all of Israel, ancient and modern. I was happy, even though my back was still painful and I had to wear the corset in spite of the heat. I would wait daily for him to come for me, until I began to see that my life was revolving entirely around him. One morning he arrived very excited and drove me to a large piece of empty land.

"This is where my art museum will be built."

"Your art museum?"

"They have just accepted my plan. I will create a vast empty space when you walk in – no stairs – only ramps going from one gallery to the next – like floating upwards."

I envied him. He knew exactly where he was going, floating upwards, whilst I was still floating around. I realised then that I didn't want to hang on to somebody else, to live someone else's dream.

"Dan, I have to go home."

"Why, Dora? I will be here for you."

"I know you will. When I find my own way, I will come back."

22

A New Way

Hardy, who was now working for Bernie and making lots more money, had found a larger, unfurnished apartment for my parents in Swabbing. He was a very good son and brother. I don't know what we would have done without him. The apartment had central heating, which meant that Papa no longer had to go down three flights of stairs each morning to bring up buckets of coal. I was very busy for a while helping Mama furnish it. She had her own chairs again, her own table, her own bed – we had our own proper home at last. We even bought a television set. I hardly ever watched it as I went out most evenings, and Mama soon decided that it put her to sleep. Papa was permanently too busy to watch. He had always loved football, he had played for the youth team of the famous Stuttgart Kickers when he had been a boy, but he preferred to watch it where the action was, rather than on a box. He had become a staunch supporter of Bayern Munich and every Saturday a car's horn would toot outside.

"Emil, Emil, are you coming?" Young men would be looking up anxiously from their car.

"Papa, where are you going with these kids?" I would ask.

"Football, of course; and then we all go for a beer."

"Why don't you go with people your own age?"

"Old, I am myself."

Mama would laugh; she let him do whatever came into his head. They had managed to discover a happy life together again. Mama would shop and cook Papa's favourite meals in her own clean kitchen. In the evening, Papa would sip his glass of half red wine, half sparkling *Sekt*, and discuss the day. Mama would then serve him his soup, which he insisted should begin every meal.

I was still in pain, especially in the mornings. The question continually hanging over me – what was I going to do with my life? Mama, as ever, finally came up with a solution.

"Bernie is coming to Dusseldorf. Why don't you talk to him?"

I took the train to Dusseldorf and met Bernie at the Schloss Hotel, where he was busy setting up and recruiting people for an IOS German operation. To my surprise, he found time for me. I don't know if Mama had spoken to him, he always respected her. She always said she had cleaned his bottom when he had been a baby. He got rid of everyone else and sat alone with me in his plush suite.

"Dora, why don't you go back on the stage?"

"Doing what? You know I can't dance anymore."

"Acting."

"Acting? I have never had a great desire to act. I don't know if I could."

"Of course you can. I have seen you dance on stage – I know you have great personality and power."

"But I've never acted. How would I go about becoming an actress?"

"I've made enquiries. The two best schools in Europe are the Reinhart School in Vienna and the Royal Academy of Dramatic Art in London."

"They will cost money. I could not afford it."

"I think I can help you. I want IOS to raise its public profile. It just so happens that we have established a fund to support young artists. You will be one of the first beneficiaries. I know you have talent and deserve it."

"Are you serious?" I didn't want to take money from him and be like all his other girls, but this was more like a grant or scholarship.

"Yes. Where would you like to go Vienna or London?"

I couldn't face Vienna, being a student where I had once been a leading dancer. London was different, a new adventure.

"London. At least I will learn to speak English."

"Great. That's settled. I have friends in London who will find someone to help you."

And so my future was decided.

23

London

"Take the world and shake it," Papa said as he gave me a farewell hug at the airport. Mama just held my hand; her eyes said everything. I had been given another chance and I knew I must make it. The plane flew into a grey cloud as it made its slow descent into London. At passport control, I was met with what I considered impertinent questions.

"How much money do you have? How long will you be staying? What do you intend to do?"

I couldn't understand. A young man behind me in the queue acted as my translator.

"I have an allowance of \$150.00 a month to live on," The other two were impossible to answer.

"You can stay three months." He stamped my passport.

"But that won't be enough. I want to study here."

"Then the school must apply for an extension for you."

Ferdy Maine was waiting on the other side of customs to take me into London. He was tall, handsome, with distinguished grey temples. He had been born in Germany, where his Jewish father had been a judge in Mainz, but Ferdy had escaped to England in 1932. I found out, many years later, that he had been a secret agent for M15 during the war. He had been an actor ever since, playing small parts, very often Nazis, in countless British films. He explained his plans for me in a perfect German.

"Dora, you must first go to a language school and learn English. In a year or so, you may be able to audition for the Royal Academy of Dramatic Art."

"A year or so? Mr Maine, I haven't got the time. When are the next auditions?"

"Next month, I have the application forms with me, but it will be impossible if you don't speak English."

I looked at the forms. I couldn't understand a single word.

"Mr Maine, could you please fill them out for me."

"I tell you again it's impossible. You must understand you must be able to speak Shakespeare. It is very, very, difficult. Even for me, and I've been here for nearly thirty years."

"I haven't got thirty years."

"Even if you speak English you still have to pass the audition. They are very selective. Hundreds try every year, very few are accepted."

It already seemed much harder than I had imagined, but I was determined not to give in.

"Can you find me a good teacher? I will work day and night. Why not try?"

He reluctantly agreed and drove me into London in his very smart Lagonda. I saw the famous London taxis, red pillar boxes, policeman in helmets, and rows and rows of identical houses, which I had seen in so many films. London had not been destroyed like Vienna and the German cities, but it was still badly scarred and in need of rejuvenation. The buildings were beautiful, but black with soot from the myriad of smoking chimneys on top of every roof. He drove me to a small private hotel, very near South Kensington tube station.

"It's not the best hotel in town, but it's very central and not expensive. I've booked you a small room."

It was indeed a small room. Small and dark and depressing; but I was used to small, depressing rooms.

Ferdy found me a teacher immediately, his friend, Milo Sperber, who had studied under Max Reinhardt in Vienna. Mr Sperber, as I always called him, was a very small bundle of nervous energy. His lively eyes were continually flickering behind his small round glasses. Like Ferdy, he had escaped to England from the Nazis, and had worked for the BBC propaganda services throughout the war. He was an actor who taught and directed at RADA, so was the ideal teacher for me. We studied the set audition speeches together – comedy and tragedy, I had to do one of each. One piece had to be from a classical play. Sperber could see that the language of Shakespeare would be impossible for me and decided on a piece of Moliere, and for the modern, a speech of Laura's from *The Glass Menagerie*. Mr Sperber explained the gist of what they meant in German and I learnt them by rote, with the same fanatical single-mindedness that I had had when learning to dance. Every morning I would go by the underground to Mr Sperber's little flat in Hampstead. I could see that he led a very lonely life and he became quite obsessed with getting me through the audition. Some afternoons I sat in the gallery of the Old Bailey; it was just as theatrical as in the movies with the barristers and judges in the wigs and robes. I listened intently, trying to catch the musical tone of their speeches, although I had no idea what they were arguing about. In the evenings, I would sit in my little dark room, with a speck of grey sky through the unwashed window, and cram the speeches and emotions into my head. The words might just as well have been Chinese if I hadn't had an open dictionary constantly beside me. Sometimes I would sit in the shabby hotel lounge and watch the black and white television, desperately trying to understand a little of what was being said and the tone of the language. Someone had told me that you could only understand a language properly when you heard it in your dreams. Every night before I went to sleep I told myself to dream in English.

The day of the audition came all too quickly. Mr Sperber said he would watch from the balcony in the small theatre and tell me how I had done. I took a taxi to Gower Street and entered RADA through the door with the stone figures of comedy and tragedy on either side, and wondered what my fate would be. A very effeminate porter, incongruously dressed in a military uniform which was much too tight for him, was waiting in the lobby. He ticked my name off on his clipboard. I asked for a toilet and took off my hated corset. I wanted to move as gracefully as possible, even if it caused me pain. I returned to the lobby where the porter showed me a bench on which to wait. I could hear perfect English voices wafting up from below. On the wall were lists of some of the famous alumni. Even I, with my complete lack of English, could distinguish Charles Laughton, John Gielgud, and Vivien Leigh, whom I had seen on stage that night in Vienna. What was I doing here? How could I ever think that I could learn to act and learn English to boot, in less than a month? But I was determined to try with every fibre of my being.

My name was called from below and I went down the stairs. Somebody passed me coming up, but I was in such a trance that I didn't notice whether it was male or female. I went through a door and stepped on to the stage of a small theatre. I could just make out three heads sitting watching me in the dark and Mr Sperber's small round spectacles glinting up above. I didn't want them to know I didn't speak English so I decided to get in first and not give them a chance to ask me questions.

"Dora Reisser. Agnes, *School for Wives* by Moliere," I announced and began straight away.

I found the small stage easy, after the large opera houses I had been used to. I was amazed how comfortable I felt. The words came out as I had learnt them. I knew how to use my eyes flirtatiously, and moved gracefully all over the small stage in what I suppose were very balletic movements. It was over very quickly. I sensed they were about to ask me questions.

"Laura, from *The Glass Menagerie*," and I plunged in again.

Mr Sperber had chosen well. I felt Laura's pain and emotions as my own. I finished and all my confidence fell away. I realised that my legs were shaking. I could hear them whispering and shuffling papers. There was no escaping his time. The man in the middle, who I later learnt was John Fernald, the Principal, cleared his throat and was about to speak to me. I was petrified. I turned and fled from that little stage like Cinderella from the ball.

I ran back up the stairs, past the next candidate coming down, again I did not notice the sex, and sank onto the bench. After the excitement of the actual audition my doubts came flooding back. How could I be so arrogant to think that I could be admitted to such a place? I went over the speeches again in my head, searching for mistakes. I was aware that someone was speaking to me. I looked up and saw a young man in a chunky sweater. He was quite rough-looking, although he had a nice smile. I shook my head. I didn't understand a word he was saying. Suddenly, angry shouts erupted from above. Mr Sperber came down the stairs from the gallery. The young man smiled and shrugged and said something to me before he hurried off.

"I told him to leave you alone. Don't have anything to do with him. He's one of the new working-class type actors that Mr Fernald wants for the new kitchen sink plays. He was saying that he hoped you would be accepted. He says that to all the girls. He just wants to get them in bed."

I didn't care about that. I had only one thing in my mind. "Did I do it right?"

His eyes twinkled. "Why are you sitting there as if the world's problems were on your shoulders? You were very good."

I jumped up. "Did I pass?"

"It will be a week or two before they finally decide; they have to see more candidates. But I would say you have a very good chance."

"Mr Sperber, I have to know as soon as possible to arrange for a student permit to stay in the country."

He rubbed his nose and heaved up his shoulders, enjoying my absolute dependence on him. "I'll see what I can do. I'll explain the circumstances to Mr Fernald. It may take a few days. Why don't you come back here on Saturday morning? I am rehearsing a production with the final students; I should have the answer by then. The Academy will be shut; ring the bell and I'll send someone to let you in."

I thanked him, but still had to endure the agony of three days uncertainty before I returned to Gower Street. Now that the ordeal of the audition was over I had time to explore London. The streets looked drab compared to Munich, there were still bomb sites everywhere, it was hard to realise that the British had won the war. They were set in their insularity; the Continent seemed to be ten years ahead. I made frequent visits to the Victoria and Albert Museum across the road from my hotel, and discovered the King's Road, which I have loved ever since. It is the first place I visit whenever I return to London. I felt at ease with the Londoners, I did not feel the undercurrent of anti-Semitism that had been so prevalent among the Viennese. I began, very slowly, to exercise again. I realised that the corset was not doing me any good. My muscles were wasting away. It would be better to bear the pain until they grew stronger.

Saturday came at last. My heart was pounding as I rang the bell. It continued pounding as I waited. I rang again before I heard the sharp crack of stiletto heels moving slowly towards me over the marble floor. There was a fumbling with the lock, the door opened an inch or so, and a face covered with pale make-up, with dark painted lips and heavy black-lined eyes appeared through the crack.

"Are you, Dora? Come in." Thank God, she spoke French. Her figure was slender, almost too skinny. "I'm Sarah Miles, Mr Sperber sent me because he says you don't speak English and I speak French. I went to a very good school. You are to come and watch the rehearsal."

Watching a rehearsal was the last thing I wanted to do. I wanted to know my fate, but she talked like a waterfall, without pausing for breath. I struggled to understand

"Have you ever watched a rehearsal? Mr Sperber is a very emotional director. We are doing *Six Characters in Search of an Author*, I'm playing the lead. I'm going to be a star when I leave RADA. My boyfriend's father, Robin Fox, is the best agent in London, and he's taking me under his wing."

She had a childlike and confident manner and led me, with her funny walk in shoes that appeared to be a size too big, along a myriad of passages to the backstage area of the Vanbrugh Theatre, and finally through a pass door into the auditorium. Mr Sperber was there, frowning at the actors on stage. I waved to him, desperate to see his reaction, but it was obvious he didn't want to be interrupted. Did that mean I hadn't been accepted? All my doubts and despair came flooding back. Mr Sperber began screaming at the actors; I hardly heard what this strange girl, Sarah, was saying.

"It's very tough here. You see, they break you down first and if you survive that, they build you up. They get rid of quite a lot during the first two terms. I was lucky, they always thought I was talented and I always got the leading parts. It's much easier to impress them when you play leading parts."

I could tell she was talented. She had the same confidence in her acting as I had had as a dancer. She appeared to have figured everything out; but I knew how quickly things can disappear.

Mr Sperber had climbed onto the stage and was now demonstrating how it should be played, acting the male and female parts. He knew all the lines. It was almost comic, especially the love scenes.

"He's a very good director," Sarah observed. "If you're lucky you'll get him in your first term."

"I don't even know if I have got in."

"Oh, didn't I tell you? You've been accepted. Mr Sperber said I was to tell you."

I could have kissed her, even though she had made me suffer. I kissed Mr Sperber when he broke for lunch.

I had made it. I was in. Acting would never be the same as my first love, ballet, but it would have to do. I had got my second chance. I would take it and shake it.

24

Postscript

David Weston: I was the boy in the chunky sweater. I met Dora again a few days after she had joined the academy and invited her for a coffee in Olivelli's in Store Street. To my surprise, she accepted. I have a suspicion her main intention was that I would help her with her Shakespeare, but we have been together, with a few breaks here and there, for more than fifty-five years.

She completed the course at RADA and left with Robin Fox as her agent. She had a very successful career throughout the sixties, including a musical with Peter Brook, who thought she could be the new Piaf, and countless films and television plays. She played Maria Oswald in the BBC's *Play of the Month*, was a regular opposite Robert Hardy in *The Trouble Shooters* and Gerald Flood in *The Rat Catchers*. She acted leading roles with Michael Bryant, Barry Foster, Ian Carmichael, Bernard Lee, Bradford Dillman and Edward Fox. She appeared in practically every TV film series that was made at that time – *The Avengers, Man in a Suitcase, Court Martial, The Saint, The Baron, Pathfinders*, and went to Hollywood with *The Dirty Dozen*.

Following the birth of her sons – as ever, she never did anything by half, having two Caesareans within eleven months of each other – she decided that she would have to have a more permanent income. She knew from her own lack of it, that education was the most important thing, and was determined to give her sons the very best. (She succeeded; both boys went to university – one to Oxford and the other to Bristol.) She embarked on her third career, as a fashion designer, with only seventy pounds and a second-hand sewing machine, and the idea of creating *haute couture* for the masses. She designed, sold and manufactured with her usual prodigious energy and determination, and within a few years had her own window in Harrods, Selfridges and Fenwick, and was the first British designer to have her own area on the designer floor at Bergdorf Goodman in New York. She designed for Dak's International, a Liberty-Reisser collection for the Far East, and originated the women's range at Austin Reed. She won the British Designer of the Year Award for Day Wear, and her label sold throughout Europe, the United States and Canada.

Dora: I had no desire ever to go back to Sofia, until during a visit to Istanbul with David in the mid-nineties, I discovered that there was a daily Orient Express service and decided, on the spur of the moment, to buy first-class return tickets from a local travel agent.

David: It wasn't the Orient Express that we had imagined, at that time it was merely a branch line between Bucharest and Istanbul, and we had a very uncomfortable trip in a very primitive train. When we arrived in Sofia I wanted to ask directions, but Dora walked on ahead by herself. I followed behind her and could only see the little girl finding her own way back from school.

Dora: I was in a trance. It was as if someone was guiding me – I must have been Mama. I came into the huge square in front of the Cathedral, where I had been nearly blown away. I went inside. Nothing had changed. The red light was still burning above the altar; the ornaments and icons were still gleaming, the air was heavy with incense. I said a little prayer to whatever God there may be for protecting me during all the years I had been away. I came out and Mama led out me of the square, on and on, through vaguely familiar streets until, around a corner, there it was, 1 Ulitsa Titscher, the building that Papa had built. His garage, one of the first private garages in Sofia, was still there beside it – a one-storey building at the end of a drive. I looked up at the windows on the first floor, and realised that that would have been the last sight Papa would have had of his beloved home that terrible morning when the Gestapo had dragged him away. I went inside and saw the door of the cellar where Hardy and I had sheltered from the bombs, and then slowly, very slowly, with my heart full of sorrow, remembering those happy days that the war had snatched away, I climbed the stairs to our home. I rang the bell, it was a different bell, and a woman opened the door.

She looked at me suspiciously. "What do you want?"
"Nothing; I used to live here."
"You must be mistaken."
"No; I used to live here. It was our home."

"I bought this apartment from a Russian officer. I have the papers."

"No we used to live here. If you go to the left there is a door to the kitchen; then there is the maid's room; then the nursery. If go straight on you come a big salon…"

"Oh, yes, yes. There was once a Jewish family here, but they disappeared."

I could feel my tears flowing down my cheeks.

"No. No. No. I am here."

Final Thoughts

It comes and goes, that's what life has taught me. One must have an anchor – it doesn't matter where or what it is. For me it was, and is, my family. I count my sons as my biggest achievements, and my four grandchildren and beautiful daughters-in-law as my greatest happiness. I have never forgotten my father's maxims: I have found my way out of many deserts; I took the world and shook it with all the strength I could muster, and I have never put myself in a ghetto. I now spend my time between a converted railway station in London and a penthouse in Tel Aviv, designed for me by my very old friend, Dan Etan – in BIG ROOMS.

Dora Reisser 2016